ID0944619

The 50 Greatest Shipwrecks

The 50 Greatest Shipwrecks

Richard M. Jones

PEN & SWORD
HISTORY

First published in Great Britain in 2021 by
Pen & Sword History
An imprint of
Pen & Sword Books Ltd
Yorkshire – Philadelphia

ISBN 978 1 39900 800 6

Typeset by Mac Style
Printed and bound by CPI Group (UK) Ltd, Croydon, CR0 4YY

Pen & Sword Books Limited incorporates the imprints of Atlas,
Archaeology, Aviation, Discovery, Family History, Fiction, History,
Maritime, Military, Military Classics, Politics, Select, Transport,
True Crime, Air World, Frontline Publishing, Leo Cooper, Remember
When, Seaforth Publishing, The Praetorian Press, Wharncliffe
Local History, Wharncliffe Transport, Wharncliffe True Crime
and White Owl.

For a complete list of Pen & Sword titles please contact

PEN & SWORD BOOKS LIMITED
47 Church Street, Barnsley, South Yorkshire, S70 2AS, England
E-mail: enquiries@pen-and-sword.co.uk
Website: www.pen-and-sword.co.uk

Or

PEN AND SWORD BOOKS
1950 Lawrence Rd, Havertown, PA 19083, USA
E-mail: Uspen-and-sword@casematepublishers.com
Website: www.penandswordbooks.com

To those who have no known grave but the sea.
You are remembered.

Contents

Introduction

There are few things that fascinate, and horrify, a reader more than the tale of a tragedy at sea, brought home in more recent years by the news coverage of the sinking of the liner *Costa Concordia* and the migrant vessel that remains nameless to this day. Two vessels of different sizes, one of them a huge luxury liner carrying thousands of people, the other an old yacht-cum-fishing vessel designed to carry ten people at the most. The irony is that the *Costa Concordia* sinking cost the lives of thirty-two people, while the small vessel crammed with migrants had a death toll of well over six hundred. The different perspectives are shocking: in the one, passengers running for the lifeboats in a scene comparable to the sinking of the *Titanic*; in the other, hundreds of lifeless corpses of poor homeless people who had been crammed onto a small boat in the hope of persuading another country to let them in to live and work. Two shipwrecks, but on such drastic and opposite ends of the spectrum.

The world continues its fascination with the stories of these ships. Each wreck was once a fine, newly built vessel, with real stories, containing real people, each of whom had families, friends, employers and lives. The coming together of a sudden and catastrophic event might lead to these stories being immortalized in print, film and, in some cases, legend. We already know about the most famous of these legends – *Titanic*, *Bismarck*, *Lusitania*, *Britannic* – but there are reportedly three million shipwrecks worldwide and each of these has a potential story as good as the rest.

So, what of these missing ships? How do you discern between a famous wreck and a not-so-famous one? What makes some of these disasters worthy of mention, to the point of gripping a reader who then wants to find out more? I first began my journey into the world of lost ships at the age of 11 and since then I have studied shipwrecks from around the world, often diving on those that are accessible, checking through archives and interviewing those who were there.

It would be impossible to truthfully dictate what the fifty most interesting wreck stories would be, but, in my opinion, those in these pages come as close as you can get to a list that is as diverse and varied as possible: a mixture of the world's worst number of deaths – both wartime and peacetime – and wrecks that register no deaths at all. I have included passenger liners, oil tankers, warships, submarines, a migrant ship and cargo ships. Each one has its own fascinating history and each one affords lessons still be learned even years later.

With the growing number of ships that are now being located on the seabed by explorers such as Dr Robert Ballard, David Mearns and the late Paul Allen, the reader can make the journey into the past simply by sitting on the living room sofa with a cup of coffee and watching the story unfold in front of them. So, for this book, we will journey into the stories of fifty ships and their demise and find out just why they are so well known, or not, in history today.

Chapter 1

Mary Rose, 1545

The city of Portsmouth in the United Kingdom has been a base of naval operations and ship building for over 500 years, and one of the ships that today takes pride of place in the Historic Dockyard tourist area is the Tudor warship, *Mary Rose*. She was built here in 1510 at the start of the reign of King Henry VIII, who would be renowned for having six wives as opposed to winning heroic battles: the only battle he seemed to famously win was the fight against the Roman Catholic Church, whereby he simply created his own religion, the Church of England, and promptly divorced his first wife. But while history would focus on his personal life, his military was somewhat revolutionary and one that was the pride of the nation, even though soldiers and sailors lived, fought and died in comparative squalor.

Completed in 1511, for thirty-four years the *Mary Rose*, named after the king's sister, would serve her country well; in that time, she was modified, built up and refurbished several times without any serious thought to what this might incur later on in her career. She could carry up to ninety-one guns and over 400 crew, although these numbers varied considerably, particularly on her final voyage.

On 19 July 1545, a fleet of French warships was seen to gather off the Isle of Wight and this was cause enough to put the English fleet to sea. One of the ships sailing out of Portsmouth that day was the *Mary Rose*, still a formidable warship, fully loaded with cannon, ammunition and crew.

But what happened next shocked all those around the Solent. As the vessel picked up speed past the harbour mouth and headed out to sea in company with the *Henri Grace à Dieu*, she suddenly heeled over to starboard. Some say that she was caught by the wind: it has recently been proved that previous rebuilding efforts had left her top-heavy.

Water began flowing in through the open gunports and the weight of everything rushing to one side trapped dozens of crewmembers against the bulkheads. On the upper deck was a series of nets that were rigged to stop anybody being able to board the ship and getting any further than there, but this now served as a death trap and in just seconds the entire ship rolled over and sank.

With hundreds of people trapped in the ship, they never stood a chance; the only survivors were those in the rigging and up the masts. Although estimates put the death toll at between 400 and 700, it was clear that only thirty-five survived. As the wretched souls clung on to the rigging that now stuck out of the Solent, the King himself watched in horror from nearby Southsea Castle. What had started out as his fleet sailing gloriously into battle had turned into a major disaster.

The wreck of the *Mary Rose* was now a hazard for any shipping and the attempts at salvaging the warship were unsuccessful; instead; they managed to move her a short distance before they broke off the masts and abandoned the operation.

Here she would lie on her starboard side for almost 300 years, until 1836, when she was discovered by fishermen who snagged their nets on an obstruction and had to summon help from local divers to help clear them. After finding out that this was the lost *Mary Rose* they arranged for several artefacts, including some of her cannon, to be recovered from the wreck and brought ashore. For several years they worked on the wreck until finally giving up and once again leaving the vessel to her watery grave.

But in the mid-twentieth century there was one man who had a dream about the shipwrecks in the Solent and was determined to find them for the sake of preserving history. Alexander McKee had already published several books on shipwrecks and became fascinated with three vessels that had gone down just a few miles away from each other – HMS *Invincible* in 1758, *Royal George* in 1782 and the *Mary Rose* in 1545.

After years of painstaking research and trawling the depths of the murky waters, he finally hit the jackpot with the *Mary Rose*, announcing his discovery in 1971 with the recovery of a piece of timber from the wreck which positively identified her as the lost Tudor warship.

But now an idea was afoot that had never before been attempted. The team now formed was named the Mary Rose Trust and they had one mission on their mind – to raise the wreck and put her on display in Portsmouth. This was not as simple as it sounded: the wreck was covered by thick mud and in a very delicate condition. Due to the fact she had landed on her starboard side and slowly rotted away, half the ship was gone with the other half buried. In a way this was fortuitous – the mud of the Solent had protected the timbers and artefacts and gave the ship a fighting chance of survival, but they would have to be extra careful.

Over the next decade tens of thousands of artefacts were photographed, catalogued, raised and preserved before being allowed to be seen by anybody other than conservationists. All the time this was happening the plan to raise the wreck was becoming more of a reality with thousands of people becoming involved in the exciting operation – including HRH The Prince of Wales who actually dived on the wreck himself at one point.

With a large frame constructed to fit the remains in, the *Mary Rose* was slowly raised a few feet and lowered into a cradle, a moment of extreme anxiety for anybody watching. Thankfully, the first phase was a success and the rest of the cradle was fitted around the wreck and attached to a floating crane. The date was 11 October 1982.

In a scene never before seen, the Solent was crowded with vessels, TV cameras, aircraft and crowds along the seafront ready for the live raising of Henry VIII's warship. With agonizing slowness, the first timbers peaked out of the water and, with the first sight of her in 437 years, the whole Portsmouth area was filled with cheers and sirens blaring as the wreck of the *Mary Rose* saw the sunlight of the twentieth century.

After a slight mishap with the crane failing on one corner, the *Mary Rose* was slowly lowered onto a barge and taken into Portsmouth harbour, arriving exactly where she had been constructed 472 years before.

Over the next few years, the ship was sprayed with water to stop the timbers from rotting, then a spraying of polyethylene glycol which replaced any water impurities within the timbers with a wax substitute. This not only treated the timbers but also made them harder and more robust, but it was not a quick process. It would be another thirty years before visitors could see her in the dry and not through a misty glass case.

Today the *Mary Rose* is upright and held in place by the same cradle that was used to salvage her. The huge museum built around her houses her thousands of artefacts which tell the story of her long career and the lives of the crew that sailed in her. Some say that the wreck of the *Mary Rose* has told us more about Tudor life than any other archaeological excavation. Alexander McKee died in 1992, but because of his hard work and dedication and his teams', the legacy of the *Mary Rose* will now live on forever.

Chapter 2

Unknown Wreck at Alderney, 1592

At the north-western tip of France lies a small cluster of islands called the Channel Islands, closer to the continent but owned by the UK. One of the largest is Alderney, the northernmost, at only three and a half miles long by one and a half miles wide, with a general population of around 2,500. Together with Jersey, Guernsey and Sark, this group of islands has seen its fair share of shipwrecks over the years, what with it being so close to the point where the English Channel becomes an extremely busy shipping lane.

The residents of Alderney have for centuries been fishermen and the small harbour is home to many a vessel that would head out and sail past the dozens of tourist yachts that frequent the shoreline every year. It was one of these fishing vessels that takes us to our next wreck.

In 1977, a local fisherman named Bertie Cosheril was around half a mile to the north of the lighthouse near a reef known as The Ledge when he snagged a random concreted object on one of his crab pots; when he finally brought it on board, he put it to one side and headed back to the island as planned. A few days later he ventured to the local museum where he presented it to see if they could tell if it was anything special. This aroused the interest of the curator but he promptly handed it back to the finder with the hope that it would be looked after if it was found to be anything actually worth keeping. After taking a hammer to the concretion and breaking away the years of growth, Cosheril was astonished by the sight of a musket before his eyes.

Speaking to some local divers, they all agreed that the site of this mysterious find was worth checking out and so together they headed out to sea. Bertie took them to where he had found the musket and when the divers descended onto the site some thirty metres down, they were astonished to find a shipwreck, complete with cannon strewn across the seabed.

With excitement building, they made further dives and retrieved pottery fragments, a clay pipe and a gaming piece. But more diving on the wreck did not take place until 1990, when further exploration of the site revealed more evidence of where the wreck had come from, even managing to date the wreck to a rough timeline of the sixteenth or seventeenth century. At one point it was even given a name, *Makeshifte*, a vessel which sank transporting arms around that time and in that area, but this was not confirmed. Later investigation showed that this was not the same ship due to differences in the description of the *Makeshifte* compared to the wreck.

Hundreds of artefacts were recovered and the discovery of the wreck was finally announced in 1992, despite it being known about for fifteen years. As people began to take the wreck seriously and knowing that it was an incredible discovery, the Alderney Maritime Trust was formed to make sure that the wreck was properly documented and the artefacts preserved and protected.

The Trust made a lot of time for research into the possible identification of the ship that now lay on the Alderney seabed and to this date they still do not have a name, but what they do have is an entry in States Papers from 1592 which described a ship coming to grief around here as 'cast away about Alderney'. It is highly likely that this is the shipwreck mentioned. According to these documents, she had been carrying dispatches from England's treasurer, Lord Burghley, to Sir John Norreys who was leading Queen Elizabeth I's forces in Brittany.

This made it the only Elizabethan wreck discovered anywhere in the world, casting her as important to maritime history as the *Mary Rose* is to the Henry VIII period. With an exact year now certain, the pieces started to fit together and the artefacts and explorations continued into the 2000s.

Amazing items recovered told the historians and archaeologists about life on board a warship of that era and how they had been preserved for over 400 years despite the notorious currents and storms that sweep the Channel Islands.

As the dives continued throughout the years, more cannon were discovered and more timbers and pottery items were recovered. The Alderney Museum put several items on display to a fascinated public and the wreck gained the attraction of Bournemouth University who did their own survey of the site and photographed new relics that had long been buried by the sands. In 2008 alone around a thousand artefacts were recovered and studied, which continued with the interest of television crews who filmed the later dives and put forward their own theories, even testing replica guns in the field to gauge their firepower. There have now been several documentaries about this wreck and the interest in her seems to grow with every telling.

It is the mystery of such a revealing wreck that has sparked the passion to learn more about her and the thought that the next artefact recovered could reveal her identity so that we can finally honour those who may or may not have gone down with her off the Alderney coast.

So, for now, it will be down to the researchers, historians, divers, archaeologists and maritime experts to continue the fine work of preserving this remarkable shipwreck, and hopefully one day we will learn more about her past and, perhaps, her name.

Chapter 3

Vasa, 1628

The Swedish capital, Stockholm, is a wealth of both royal and maritime history and for hundreds of years it has seen every type of ship come and go in sight of the palace of its ruling royal family. The twists and turns of the waterways out to the open Baltic Sea proved a task in itself to navigate safely, and it would be inevitable that ships would come to grief around here, given the enormity of the task.

But for the King's own brand-new warship, *Vasa*, it wouldn't be the land masses that caused her to come to grief – she wouldn't get that far in the first place.

Built as the flagship of the Swedish Navy and launched in 1627, she was finally ready to put to sea the following year, with high hopes from all who had constructed her. At 226 feet long and displacing 1,210 tons, she could carry 300 soldiers and 145 sailors as well as 64 large guns.

This amount of armament needed two gundecks, with cannon jutting out of the openings adorned with ornate carvings of lions' heads on the gunport covers. Elsewhere, the intricacy of the artwork that graced the entire stern section was one to be marvelled at. This masterpiece displayed the royal coat of arms, figures in beautiful, bright pink and red colours, with yellows and blues mixed into the depictions of Roman emperors and various other figures. Even before going into battle she would be stared at by people with mouths agape.

After the building was completed it was time to send the largest and most powerful ship in the King's navy to sea, and on 10 August 1628 she was ready at her berth in Stockholm to wow the crowds as she sailed past. The first task was to take the ship over to a nearby naval base where she would take on supplies and any other personnel required for her first trip out into the Baltic. On board were guests of the crew and family members.

As the *Vasa* slowly edged her way from the harbour wall, sails were set and, although it was a very calm day, a slight breeze caused her to drift ever so slowly out into the deeper water. Thousands cheered and waved as this beautiful sailing art palace got around 1,700 yards away as she started to list to her port side, before righting herself. She then caught another gust and heeled over again. But what the crowds couldn't see was that water had already started to flood into the ship through the open gunports and the extra sudden weight of water was slowly making the ship heavier and more unstable. Within just a few minutes the entire lower decks of the *Vasa* were flooded and she sank like a stone in front of a shocked city, survivors scrambling out of the ship for the safety of dry land which was still so very close.

The hull of the vessel came to rest upright in thirty-two metres of water, her upper masts still protruding above the surface in a tragic re-enactment of the sinking of the *Mary Rose* eighty-three years earlier. Those who managed to escape the hull clung to the masts in the hope that help was on its way. Boats managed to rescue most of them with others managing the short swim to shore, but thirty of her crew and guests perished.

The cause of the disaster was thought to be the seriously bad design of the vessel with the gunports too close to the waterline and, being open, instantly allowing water in at an astonishing rate. If they had even made it out into the Baltic, let alone to battle against another ship, they wouldn't have stood a chance.

The wreck of the *Vasa* was now a hazard to shipping within the harbour and it needed to be salvaged straight away, so a team of salvage experts attempted to raise her from the harbour and bring her back to shore. This would be done by barges and pontoons, using the tide as a way to raise her by tightening ropes under the hull and when the tide came in, to sail it towards the next shallow area where the process would be repeated.

This was good in theory but all that was achieved was getting her stuck further into the mud and breaking off her masts. During the 1600s over fifty cannon were salvaged before the wreck was left alone and over the years completely forgotten about, other than by the few people who tried to claim salvage over the following centuries.

In the 1950s, the archaeologist and engineer Anders Franzen began a quest to locate the wreck by towing a hook and dragging it up and down Stockholm harbour in the hope of finding the last resting place of the ship that he had read so much about. He was rewarded in 1956 when, after extensive searching and painstaking research, he finally located an object that was later confirmed to be old timber. When he sent divers to investigate later that year, it was confirmed that it was indeed a ship and that it had two decks with square openings all along the side. This verified that he had found the *Vasa*.

He now put forward a plan to raise the vessel and, instead of using her for breaking up the timber and the scrap-metal value of the guns, she would instead be taken back to shore and displayed in a museum near whence she had originally set sail. For five years teams of divers, engineers and archaeologists worked hard in pitch-black water and freezing temperatures to burrow holes under the wreck of the *Vasa* in order to pass steel cables underneath, which in turn would be passed up to a pair of lifting pontoons positioned one either side of the wreck. The aim was to salvage the ship exactly as had been tried back in the days after she had sunk, only this time they had more technology and the experience of time on their side.

In 1959 the first lift began and the ship was carried slowly across the harbour and lowered again for divers to prepare her for the final lift the following year. With all the checks done and the ship safe to move, that day came on 24 April 1961 when once again thousands crowded the shore to watch the *Vasa*, only this time they would be joined by millions who would see the raising of this magnificent warship on their televisions.

Sure enough, the initial timbers broke the surface for the first time in 333 years, slowly rising out of her watery grave and, incredibly, floating on her own keel once all the water had dispersed. The *Vasa* was then taken over to a dry dock where she ended her journey that had started three centuries before just a few hundred yards away.

The incredible artefacts found on the *Vasa* told researchers so much more about the Swedish navy of the seventeenth century than first thought; they even found several victims whose bones were reconstructed and laid out on display.

Today the ship and all her treasures are on display at the Vasamuseet in Stockholm, visited by 1.5 million visitors every year; it is one of the most visited museums in Scandinavia. The ship today stands proud within the enclosure of her museum, with all the lion-head carvings on display and her masts standing high, as if ready to sail back out to sea once again to continue her voyage that was so suddenly interrupted all those years ago.

Chapter 4

Bonhomme Richard, 1779

The United States of America is today a superpower with the most powerful navy in the world, but who would have thought that it was originally led by a Scotsman who had earned the title 'Father of the American Navy' by the time he died?

John Paul was born on 6 July 1747 in Kirkbean on the south-western edge of Scotland, and from the age of 13 he was already going out to sea, learning the ropes and traditions that would be the start of an amazing maritime career.

By the age of 23 he had already been in command of several merchant vessels but two incidents occurred that involved mutinous sailors and corpses. He was arrested for the first incident and released on bail, but the second caused him leave Britain for good and flee to America, changing his name by adding the surname Jones.

It was here in America in 1775 that he decided to sign up for the navy who were at the moment fighting the War of Independence against Britain, and he was more than happy to fight against the country of his birth. Within three years he had shown great leadership and fighting spirit in the various missions he had been involved in, but, in 1778, he went one step further by attacking the west coast of Britain on board his ship, the *Ranger*. After his crew went ashore and raided the town of Whitehaven and attempted to kidnap the Earl of Selkirk near his hometown, he then returned to France triumphant.

A year later he had been given a new ship, an ex-East Indiaman vessel called *Duc de Duras* which he renamed *Bonhomme Richard*, in tribute to the work of Benjamin Franklin. He set sail and headed once again to the British coast to see what trouble could be had and hopefully give the Royal Navy a run for their money.

On 23 September 1779, the fleet, consisting of the *Bonhomme Richard*, *Pallas*, *Vengeance* and *Alliance*, was cruising south down the East Yorkshire coast when they came upon a convoy on the horizon led by the frigate HMS *Serapis* and armed escort ship *Countess of Scarborough.*

As the British ships saw the Americans on the horizon, the reality of their opponents being the enemy coming in for an attack dawned on them and so they ordered the convoy to disperse while the two British warships prepared for action.

That evening the two fleets met off Flamborough Head. As they came within range, the *Serapis* opened fire followed by the *Vengeance,* and before long all the ships were firing at each other. The locals from the town of Bridlington and all the way along the cliffs at Flamborough were lined up watching this incredible naval battle taking place just a few miles from their homes.

The ships were slowly drifting towards each other, the cannon shots blasting huge holes in the sides of the ships. The *Bonhomme Richard* and *Serapis* looked like they were going to collide, but this was Jones bringing his ship close enough to lock the two vessels together where the crews would shoot each other down with muskets and even cannons.

The ships were a mess of body parts, splintered wood, fires and explosions but neither Jones nor Richard Pearson of the *Serapis* would yield. When asked to surrender, Jones simply shouted back, 'I have not yet begun to fight!' which has today gone down in history as his most famous quote.

The other ships in the battle were hard at each other with the *Countess of Scarborough* firing at the *Pallas,* but when the *Alliance* joined that fight, it was soon apparent that it was a no-win situation and the *Countess* surrendered, but not before *Alliance* had fired upon the two other ships locked together, causing damage to both friend and foe.

As the crew of *Bonhomme Richard* boarded the *Serapis* under heavy fire from both *Serapis* and again, the *Alliance,* the frigate was soon taken over and the British captain accepted that further fighting would achieve nothing but more bloodshed, and surrendered. It was not long after this that Jones realized just how badly damaged the *Bonhomme Richard* was and that holding out for any longer just may have seen the American ship sink from under him, but hindsight could not be relied upon.

The crew and supplies from the *Bonhomme Richard* were transferred over to *Serapis* and although they would fight to keep her afloat, she was not going to make it: the *Bonhomme Richard* was allowed to sink somewhere between twenty-four and forty-eight hours after the battle had ended, somewhere in the North Sea.

The American fleet then sailed to Texel in Holland where Jones became an American and French hero and has been a legend ever since. The *Serapis* would later end her life in the waters off Madagascar after a fire engulfed the ship and she sank along with eight of her crew.

Jones would later go on to become an admiral in the Russian navy, be accused of rape, and then be given a new job as US Consul in France. On 18 July 1792, he was found dead in a Paris apartment, buried a few miles away and then forgotten about. In the early 1900s President Theodore Roosevelt sent a team of experts to try and locate his body and, after a painstaking search, they finally located his remains in an unmarked grave. The body was exhumed in 1905 and shipped back to the United States where he is today interred within the Naval Academy at Maryland, in a tomb fit for an admiral. A statue of John Paul Jones also stands near the Lincoln Memorial in Washington DC.

The wreck of the *Bonhomme Richard* is one of the greatest shipwrecks that has still never been found, but this is not through lack of trying. Adventure author Clive Cussler has undertaken four expeditions, in 1978, 1979, 1984 and 2004, three of which featured in his writings, particularly in his non-fiction account, *The Sea Hunters*, and later the documentary of the same name that covered his last expedition which sailed out of Whitby. But with thousands of dollars spent, he came away empty-handed.

Dozens of divers and fishermen over the years have claimed to have located the wreck but nobody has actually found definitive proof that any of them are anything but merchant vessels or sailing ships that have been wrecked on this coast – and there are thousands of them littered across the seabed. Some have been legitimate discoveries that show promise; others are nothing more than driftwood from attention seekers who want their names in the papers.

The only other serious searches were done by the Ocean Technology Foundation in 2006 that conducted Sonar sweeps of the area where they believed the ship went down. Year after year they came back with bigger and better technology including the NR-1 nuclear research submarine and each year they found several targets but have never announced a discovery of anything relating to the *Bonhomme Richard*. Being rebranded the Global Foundation for Ocean Exploration, their last survey was in 2016 after a continual effort almost every year since they started.

But for now, the story of the *Bonhomme Richard* ends with the tomb of Jones in Maryland and the birthplace museum in Kirkbean. For the ship that made him famous there is a toposcope on the tip of Flamborough Head near the lighthouse showing where the battle took place and where one of the most incredible sea fights took place in front of an audience of thousands.

Chapter 5

Waratah, 1909

There are many mysteries of the sea, some of them household names such as the *Mary Celeste*, Flight MH370 and the *Flying Dutchman*, but one of the most baffling of these is the disappearance of the passenger ship *Waratah* off South Africa in 1909, without a trace of her or the 211 people on board.

This Blue Anchor liner was just over 9,000 gross tons and 465 feet long, designed for the England–South Africa–Australia route with both passengers and cargo. With the technology on board, she could travel at around 13 knots and make the journey in around five or six weeks, depending on the weather of course. Launched on 12 September 1908 at Whiteinch, Scotland, *Waratah* was on her sea trials in just a month and very soon ready to ply the long route around the world the same day as the trials were completed.

She sailed on her maiden voyage on 5 November 1908 and arrived in Adelaide on 15 December, with a stop-off at Cape Town on the way. Her journey back early the following year took two months, after which she was inspected in dry dock and underwent some minor repair work.

Her second voyage began on 27 April 1909 and she arrived in Adelaide on 6 June where she began preparations for the return journey back to Britain via Sydney, Melbourne and again Adelaide, before heading across the Indian Ocean to Durban and Cape Town, arriving in Durban on 25 July. At this point, in Durban, there was a strange incident whereby a passenger reported having strange visions and felt that he was not happy with the state of the ship, that she felt 'top heavy' in the seas. He promptly left the ship, convinced that this was a message to get off while he still could.

She sailed as planned on 26 July 1909, heading to Cape Town which would be her final stop before commencing her journey to London. The following day she was proceeding at her normal speed without any visible problem, and several sightings of her were noted by passing ships as the day started to bring rougher weather in the ship's direction.

By the evening of the 27th, heavy seas and strong winds were causing havoc with shipping, with some reporting some of the worst storms ever witnessed, all the while trying to navigate the southern coast of South Africa, struggling to keep upright in monstrously high waves. It was probably obvious by this point that the *Waratah* would be late getting into port, but as it happened that would be the least of anyone's worries. For she was never seen again.

The ship was due into Cape Town on 29 July but when she was reported as overdue, it didn't cause too much concern as that was normal for ships in those days, especially after a violent storm had been tossing them around for two days, and where they could have been forced off course by miles.

But when no word came of her, and other ships which had taken the same route made it into port, concern started to grow for the fate of the ship.

On 1 August 1909, the first search teams were dispatched on a tug to search for any trace of the *Waratah*; the Royal Navy warships HMS *Pandora* and HMS *Forte* were also deployed to head further out but the weather was still so horrendous that the *Forte* suffered damage and had to put into dry dock on her return.

But the search was all in vain as ship after ship reported nothing to suggest that *Waratah* had even been in the area. Hopes that she had broken down and was adrift faded, and after four months the search was officially called off, a further privately funded search paid for by the relatives again came up with nothing.

Over the last century there have been numerous sightings of wreckage, bodies and other unidentified items from the *Waratah*, but none of this could ever be confirmed or officially linked to the ship. The ship had simply vanished off the coast of South Africa without a trace, with all her 211 passengers and crew.

There have been many theories about what happened; an inquiry was set up in 1910 to establish the facts and see if anything could be gleaned from examining the evidence. The focus was on her instability reported by the fleeing passenger who gave testimony to the struggle she had had to stay upright, backed up by several others who had noticed the same issue on previous voyages. The inquiry also found that the ships purporting to have seen her in her last twenty-four hours would have put the ship in impossible positions so some of them had to have been mistaken.

But at the end of it all no one to this day has any idea of what happened and although there are theories such as the weather, a freak wave, fire/explosion, capsize and even a whirlpool, there is not a shred of evidence to support any of these and they remain just that – theories.

One person who was more than happy to put the effort in to solve the mystery was explorer Emlyn Brown who launched a series of searches for the wreck from the early 1980s right up until 1999 when he made an exciting announcement that he believed he had found the wreck of the *Waratah*. The press made the discovery public and he believed that he had finally solved the mystery of what had befallen the ship, until a proper exploration was done of the remains of what he had found in 2001 and the truth of what he had found came to light. Although he had indeed made a shipwreck discovery, what he actually found was the wreck of the *Nailsea Meadow*, a cargo ship sunk by a German submarine in 1943 en route to Egypt. Although it was disappointing, he continued the quest until finally giving up in 2004 after exhausting all his search areas.

Today the disappearance of the *Waratah* still remains one of those mysteries of the sea that has never been solved and, until the wreck is found and examined, we will never know what happened to her on that stormy voyage over a century ago.

Chapter 6

Titanic, 1912

I t would be impossible to write a book on the fifty greatest shipwrecks without mentioning the most famous of them all, the RMS *Titanic*. While there are already thousands of books written about the sinking of this luxury liner, not to mention TV and film appearances, the entire story of the *Titanic* seems never ending. With many aspects of the liner's loss covered in every way imaginable, it leaves me to present a brief outline of her story.

It was 1907 at a dinner party that the heads of the two great businesses came together to discuss the construction of three magnificent liners. They would be the largest and most luxurious ships that had ever graced the waves and they would be the pride of the White Star Line. The Belfast-based shipbuilder Harland & Wolff would deliver the 46,000-gross-ton *Olympic*, followed by the *Titanic* and later the *Britannic*, each of their triple screws powering their huge bulks through the seas at around 23 knots, their four towering funnels leaving anyone who viewed them awestruck.

After the *Olympic* was successfully launched in 1910 and placed into service, her sister the *Titanic* followed on 31 May 1911 and spent the next ten months being fitted out in dry dock before completing her sea trials and heading down to the south coast of England, to the port of Southampton.

On 10 April 1912, the ship sailed with over 2,200 people on board, not completely full but enough for there to be a huge fanfare of excitement like there had been with the *Olympic* the previous year. As she moved away from the dockyard and headed out into Southampton Water, her suction pulled the liner *New York* away from her mooring and caused several securing lines to snap. It was only the quick-thinking tug masters who prevented a collision, the smaller liner being tugged out of the way as the *Titanic* resumed her journey.

On board was the height of society, millionaires rubbing shoulders with tycoons in First Class, immigrants seeking a better life in Third Class, and everyone in between. The ship made two further stops at the French port of Cherbourg that evening and Queenstown in Ireland the following day. As she sailed off into the Atlantic, few realized that she would never been seen again.

For several days she transited without much incident, a fire in a coal bunker being the only noteworthy event but this was extinguished as the coal was used up over time. By the evening of Sunday, 14 April, she had made good progress and had delighted her passengers in every way.

For the crew, they had to keep a sharp eye out when they came on watch. Ice had been reported by other ships, with warnings being picked up by the radio room staff on their new wireless equipment.

At 2340 that night, lookouts in the crow's nest spotted an iceberg looming in the distance. With three rings of the bell, the bridge was informed and the officer of the watch threw the ship hard over to port in order to avoid it. But it was too late – the ship scraped by which was enough for the underwater spar of the iceberg to punch holes in the side of the ship for several hundred feet.

The ship had always boasted of the safety features that were the watertight doors, but they only went up to a few decks and then suddenly stopped, meaning the water would simply flow over the top and fill up the next compartment as the ship's bow got heavier. Within minutes the designer Thomas Andrews told Captain Edward Smith that his ship had not long left to live.

Over the next two hours the events that surround the sinking are etched into legend, with the romance of elderly husbands and wives who refused to leave each other, the owner climbing into a lifeboat and then having to spend the rest of his life justifying his decision, officers pulling out guns to keep the crowds from swamping the decks, all the while as the ship got lower and lower.

At 0220 on the morning of Monday, 15 April 1912, the *Titanic* took her final dive and disappeared beneath the waves, taking over 1,500 people with her. The 705 survivors were eventually rescued by the smaller liner *Carpathia* which had turned around when her radio operator heard the distress signals. Another liner, the *Californian*, had stopped for the night in ice and couldn't move, her radio operator being asleep and not hearing about it until the following day.

As the questions were being asked as to how so many people could die on board the largest and most advanced liner in the world, it soon became apparent just how arrogant everybody had been. The press had called her 'unsinkable' yet the lifeboats only had space for half the people on board (a loophole in the regulations that allowed the owners to only put up the bare minimum). Binoculars meant for the lookouts were locked away which meant that they didn't see the iceberg in time. Officers on the *Californian* who saw the distress rockets did nothing when they could have woken the radio operator and got the full story straight away. This was a wakeup call for the owners of such liners; the inquiries were scathing and many lessons were learned – the hard way.

But for the *Titanic* herself, the dream of finding the wreck all started when the book and film *A Night to Remember* ignited passions in many. By the 1980s serious expeditions were under way to conduct a search for the missing liner. Three expeditions by Texan oil millionaire Jack Grimm led to nothing.

But it took Dr Robert Ballard from the Woods Hole Oceanographic Institute, along with a second French exploration team from IFREMER, to finally locate the wreck, on 1 September 1985. Grainy photographs showed her fo'c'sle and upper deck, not much to go on but enough to show the world that the *Titanic* was indeed found.

In July 1986, Ballard returned with a new research vessel and a submersible named *Alvin*, which had already proved its worth in several incredible discoveries on previous expeditions. The images and video footage the team brought back stunned the world. The *Titanic* had broken in two and the huge sections were over 1,000 yards apart from each other.

Since she was found there have been many more expeditions, some of them retrieving thousands of artefacts and even pieces of the hull that had broken off, lying in the huge debris field separating the bow from the stern. These have been preserved and displayed in museums around the world and have told many new and interesting stories about the people who sailed on *Titanic*.

But the wreck is slowly collapsing as an expedition found out in 2019, although she is still in surprisingly good condition, and while ever the wreck is not ripped apart by salvagers, she may remain that way for a long time yet.

With memorials built to the victims in Southampton, Belfast, New York, Washington, Cherbourg and Cobh (Queenstown), it is doubtful that the story of the *Titanic* will ever really fade away.

Chapter 7

Empress of Ireland, 1914

After the loss of the *Titanic* the world would never believe that in just two years there would be another liner disaster that would have such a huge death toll, but in 1914 it was the *Empress of Ireland* that hit the headlines following a tragic set of circumstances leading to her demise.

The Atlantic route for ocean liners was becoming more and more popular and the Canadian Pacific Steamship Company wanted a piece of the action and ordered two new liners to be built – the *Empress of Ireland* and the *Empress of Britain*. These two ships would give the White Star and Cunard Lines something to think about in terms of luxury and size.

The *Empress of Ireland* was the second of the two to be launched from the Fairfield Shipbuilding yard in Govan, Scotland, on 27 January 1906, two months after her sister ship had taken to the water. At 570 feet long and with capacity for over 1,500 passengers in four classes (first, second, third and steerage), she carried a crew of almost 400.

Her transatlantic route would take the ship from Liverpool to Quebec; she began her career at times over capacity in the various classes, stopping at various Canadian ports along the way to drop off passengers, mail and cargo.

By 1914 she was making the same journeys as always under the command of Captain Henry Kendall who had become famous in 1910 when he was in charge of the SS *Montrose*: he ordered a radio transmission alerting the authorities that a suspected murderer wanted by the police might have boarded. After taking a faster ship and overtaking the *Montrose*, Dr Hawley Crippen was arrested in Canada and hanged for the murder of his wife.

Now, on the morning of 29 May 1914, Captain Kendall was less than a month into his new command, taking his ship on the regular journey from Quebec to Great Britain with the liner slowly moving up the St

Lawrence River, no different to what she had done countless number of times before. Disembarking the pilot at Rimouski, she continued her journey upriver.

In the opposite direction and inbound to Quebec was the Norwegian collier *Storstad*, which was about to complete a journey from Australia and would soon be picking up her pilot for the last leg of the voyage. At 440 feet long, she was a lot smaller than the liner, but it would soon be apparent that size didn't matter when it came to what happened next.

As the two vessels steamed towards each other, lights from each ship were seen in good time and both ships signalled the other their course intentions before they soon started losing each other in thick fog that suddenly enveloped them.

Continuing their courses and confident that they would pass clear, they were both shocked to find that at around 0200 hours they were so close that a collision was inevitable. *Storstad*'s bow slammed into the starboard midships of the *Empress of Ireland*, badly damaging the sides enough to open the hull to the sea at an alarming angle. Water rushed in and she took on an immediate list.

The sudden collision took everybody by surprise, not least by it being at such an early hour. The watertight doors were not shut in time and hundreds of people rushed for the lifeboats but found that the list was so severe so quickly that most of the lifeboats couldn't be launched at all, with only a few managing to get off the ship, with the rest hanging useless.

As the liner slowly rolled over onto her starboard side, the *Storstad* lowered her boats and began to rescue those in the water and attempted to get as many people as possible on board. Several other ships nearby raced to the scene following the distress call made by the *Empress* and were met by the pilot vessel *Eureka* and mail ship *Lady Evelyn*.

The struggle to get off the sinking liner would be in vain for many people because just fourteen minutes after the collision, the *Empress of Ireland* rolled onto her side and sank. Hundreds of people were now stranded in the middle of the river in the pitch blackness, hoping that one of the ships would be able to see them and haul them to safety.

When the final count was confirmed, 1,012 people were dead – 840 passengers and 172 crew – with survivors on the rescue ships totalling 465 (248 crew and 217 passengers). This was Canada's worst-ever peacetime maritime disaster.

An inquiry was set up in Quebec to find out what happened that night, presided over by Lord Mersey who had previously led the inquiry into the loss of *Titanic* two years before. After hearing from witnesses on both sides, they came to the conclusion that the *Storstad* had changed course and therefore was at fault in the collision. A Norwegian inquiry exonerated their collier and instead blamed the captain of the *Empress*.

The *Storstad* needed major repairs following the disaster, her crumpled bow showing the signs of the violence of the crash but incredibly she was still afloat and continued plying her voyages for several more years. She was sunk during the First World War after a torpedo from a German U-boat got her off Fastnet Rock on 8 March 1917, with three of her crew lost.

The wreck of the *Empress of Ireland* is still in remarkably good condition considering that she only lies forty metres down on the bed of the St Lawrence River. Lying on her starboard side, she was salvaged straight away with some of her cargo and bodies recovered by divers who made a hole in the exposed port side to gain access.

Canadian historians nearby have made every effort since she sank to protect her history and display the artefacts that have been salvaged from her in local museums. This has not stopped sport divers taking souvenirs and slowly stripping the wreck of anything valuable over the years, including the bones of some of the dead.

One of those who salvaged many artefacts was Philippe Beaudry who founded the Empress of Ireland Historical Society and a museum dedicated to the ship displaying all her historic treasures. In 1999 the Quebec government officially declared the wreck protected from salvage of any kind although this was not intended to stop divers enjoying a visit to the wreck and exploring her remains.

Today the hundreds of artefacts that have been raised from the wreck are now on display following the commemoration of the centenary of her sinking. The items include the brass bell bearing her name, telegraphs, furniture, crockery and bottles. It is clear now that the passion for researching this once-forgotten disaster is as strong as ever as long as people remember that this ship is not only a fascinating slice of history but also a mass grave for over 1,000 people. If people learn to respect the wreck and leave her alone, then the *Empress of Ireland* will remain virtually intact at the bottom of the river for many years to come.

Chapter 8

Lusitania, 1915

Of all the shipwrecks in the world, the name *Lusitania* still conjures up images of the horrors of the First World War, as well as the hidden mysteries that still surround the sinking of this huge liner. Even today there are still many unanswered questions about her role and the events leading up to her demise.

Originally designed for the transatlantic crossings, her owners, the Cunard Line, wanted a pair of ships that would be the fastest the world had ever seen, adding to that element of luxury that would intertwine within and make any passenger feel as if they were not on a voyage at all but in a hotel of the finest calibre.

The pair would be the *Lusitania* and the *Mauritania*, each ship with four funnels towering high above the tallest deck with a speed of 25 knots that could push the 787-foot-long vessel through the waves and across to America in just a few days.

Launched on 7 June 1906, the *Lusitania* made her maiden voyage in September the following year and immediately became one of the most popular and sought-after ships to travel on, having room for around 2,200 passengers and 850 crew housed within her spacious cabins, elegant suites and fine dining restaurants.

On her second voyage in October 1907 she won the coveted Blue Riband trophy for the fastest Atlantic crossing which she did in 4 days, 19 hours and 53 minutes. She would go on to break the eastbound record three more times and once westbound. As the years went by and her sister ship *Mauritania* entered service, they proved to be the most reliable ships on the ocean, but a little-known fact was that these ships were funded by a British government deal that meant they would be built to their specifications in order to be used in a wartime situation as auxiliary cruisers.

Few could have predicted just how close to the mark they would come at the outbreak of the war in August 1914. It was decided that *Mauritania* would be used as a troopship but *Lusitania* would remain on commercial service. Both ships had new colour schemes applied with *Mauritania* daubed in dazzle camouflage and *Lusitania* covered in warship grey paint. Both were listed as Armed Merchant Cruisers and were now ready for war.

On the *Lusitania's* 202nd voyage, she departed from New York's Pier 54 on 1 May 1915 under the cloud of a warning that had appeared in a number of newspapers stating, 'Travellers intending to embark on the Atlantic voyage are reminded that a state of war exists between Germany and her allies and Great Britain and her allies' and suggested that anybody boarding the *Lusitania* should 'do so at their own risk', referring to the area around the British Isles that had recently been declared by Germany as a 'war zone', where any ship caught in the area would be sunk without warning. It was not surprising: U-boats had been sinking cargo ships for almost a year now but had always allowed safe passage of the crews. That all changed when merchantmen began arming themselves with deck guns and attacking the submarines in turn. Now the German Navy targeted everybody without warning.

For the *Lusitania's* passengers they didn't seem too worried as the week-long journey went without incident and even as they approached land the war seemed so far away from their lives. But hidden off the Old Head of Kinsale was the submarine *U-20* and her captain Kapitänleutnant Walther Schwieger who had already sunk three cargo ships nearby. He had only a few torpedoes left but had decided to stay around and see if he could sink something else.

He must have thought his luck was in when the huge shape of the *Lusitania* appeared on the horizon in the early afternoon of 7 May 1915. Preparing a torpedo ready to fire, he couldn't believe it when the ship he was watching suddenly turned across him and gave him the perfect target lined up.

At 1410 hours he fired one torpedo and watched its progress through the periscope. What happened next shocked even the U-boat commander.

Several witnesses on the ship saw the streak coming quickly on her starboard side before a huge explosion shot water into the air just aft of the bridge. But seconds later a much larger, secondary explosion rocked the ship and sent a cloud of black dust and wreckage skywards. The *Lusitania* immediately lurched to starboard and began taking on large volumes of water, the passengers running onto the upper deck to try and escape from what was now a sinking ship in a war zone.

Swinging outwards, the starboard side lifeboats were useless: too far to jump across to; and with the port side ones swinging inwards across the deck, few could be got away. People were launched into the water while others jumped and clung on to wreckage. In a sight that shocked everybody, both on board the ship and the submarine, with several being able to see it thirteen miles away from the Irish clifftops, the ship's stern rose high into the air and then went down, leaving thousands in the sea. The entire drama had taken just eighteen minutes from beginning to end.

Local fishing vessels that had heard of the disaster sped to the scene, rescuing people out of the water and crowding their decks with terrified passengers and crew. When the final count was made public, it was found that 1,197 people had lost their lives, with 763 survivors. (These figures have been recently researched and found that initial lists counted the same person twice as well as not taking into account four stowaways.)

Immediately there was a huge outcry: how could a German submarine attack an unarmed liner and kill innocent women and children, Americans too? Did they not know it was mass murder to do so? The controversy and conspiracies began immediately with talk of two torpedoes hitting the ship and that the ship was carrying munitions and explosives. The entire episode very nearly dragged America into the war on the side of Great Britain but the Germans quickly declared an end to war-zone sinkings, which calmed the Americans down for the moment. This was later retracted and the USA entered the war in 1917 following the German continuation of unrestricted submarine warfare.

Either way, nothing could change the event and an official inquiry blamed the Germans for the sinking. But the biggest mystery was what had caused the second explosion as Schwieger was adamant that he had only fired one torpedo and certainly didn't expect to sink her.

The wreck of the *Lusitania* was discovered in 1935 using some of the earliest diving equipment and has been visited many times in the years since. One of the best surveys of the wreck was conducted in 1993 by Dr Robert Ballard who found many interesting things around the debris field. After consulting with experts, he came to the conclusion that it was not munitions that had sunk the ship, but the igniting of the coal dust which lay thick within the empty bunkers following a week at sea. The torpedo hitting the ship would have thrown a cloud of coal dust into the air that seconds later caused a catastrophic explosion, enough to sink one of the world's largest liners in just eighteen minutes.

With diving technology getting more advanced every year, there have now been several expeditions to the remains of the ship which still lies on her starboard side, the decks and bulkheads slowly collapsing in on each other, but the images and artefacts brought back up tell a story of a liner of such magnificence that few that would ever follow in her footsteps again. Such is now the legacy of the *Lusitania*.

Chapter 9

Endurance, 1915

Perhaps one of the greatest survival stories ever written about is that of which befell the crew of the barque *Endurance* during one of the most epic voyages ever attempted in one of the most inhospitable places on the planet.

She had been built in Norway in 1912 to accommodate hunting parties on the Arctic ice, and her hull had been built to withstand more than what the average ship could endure should she have to undertake such voyages. At just 144 feet long, she had both steam and sail capabilities that could propel her at a speed of a reasonable 10 knots. Being sold to explorer Ernest Shackleton before she had ever finished fitting out, he brought her to Britain and had her refitted to his specifications in order to take a crew with aims of heading to the southern hemisphere to explore the Antarctic.

Endurance sailed from Plymouth on 6 August 1914 and after a long voyage via Argentina and South Georgia, she finally reached the area of her destination by the following January, a tiresome and stormy journey for a ship with only twenty-eight men on board. But the ice was starting to slow her down and before long it was noticed that the ship was completely static, not even drifting. She was now officially trapped in the ice, not a huge worry as most ships just free themselves over time as the ice naturally breaks apart, to continue on their voyages.

But the ice didn't break apart. The hopes of drifting with the ice were dashed and Shackleton ordered the ship shut down to save her fuel and human effort. As the weeks passed, it was found that the ice and the ship were indeed slowly moving but nothing appreciable. Breaks in the ice came and went but none was sufficient for the ship to break free and move. All they could do was sit and wait.

The slow crushing of the *Endurance* took until October 1915, when ice formed around the vessel, then released her, took hold again, then banged into her before forming up around her once again. The strength of the ice against the hull bent large timbers like they were made of rubber, the sound of the groaning and creaking becoming ever louder as the timbers finally parted and allowed water to seep, then flow, into her lower decks.

Despite the pumps working hard, Shackleton ordered all supplies and the boats moved onto the ice as the situation on board became all the more desperate. On 25 October 1915, the vessel was once again hit by a large amount of built-up pressure that crushed the hull, parts being torn away and buckled. The ship was well and truly sinking but at such a slow pace that the men could go back and forth on board to retrieve things required to survive on the ice.

The next four weeks saw the ship slowly sink that little bit more each day. The rigging and masts were collapsing and the groans of the ship being bent backwards and forwards were heard by everybody there. Finally, on the afternoon of 21 November, she made her final lurch and was engulfed by the ice for one last time. The demise of the ship was captured on camera over the final few weeks by the expedition photographer whose images later became world-famous.

But now the *Endurance* expedition had to face a new dilemma. They were at the bottom of the world stranded on the most desolate location anybody could dream of. How were they going to get out of this? Shackleton's plan was to camp on the ice and drift with the pack towards an island where he knew some stores were being kept. But after several months and not far away from the destination, the ice floe broke up and the men were forced to take to the lifeboats and head to the nearest land via sea.

The three small boats arrived at Elephant Island five days later, nearly 350 miles from where their ship had sunk five months previously. This island was solid ground but it was still inhabited and there was no chance of ever being rescued there, so Shackleton took the decision to plan a journey by using just one of the boats, a 20-foot-long lifeboat he named *James Caird*, along with five men whom he considered vital to the success of the perilous journey ahead.

On 24 April 1916, the boat sailed for South Georgia, with enough supplies on board to last four weeks and hopefully enough to make the 720-mile journey without a major problem. The six crew battled strong waves over the next two weeks that had already sunk a ship in the area, when they finally came upon their destination where they rode out the storm before attempting to land safely.

It took another day before they were able to get onto the island. Only, they had landed on the uninhabited side. This forced them to set up camp once again and plan the last leg of the journey overland. Leaving three of the team behind, Shackleton and two others slowly made their way across the thirty-two miles of mountainous terrain which took them thirty-six hours. Cold, hungry, exhausted and looking older than they could ever imagine, Shackleton finally arrived at the whaling station on Stromness on 20 May 1916.

Their sorry state meant that the people at the station did not recognize them as being the same people they had seen just two years before. The shock of finally realizing that Shackleton was alive, and out there was the rest of his crew, sent a shockwave around the world as this momentous tale of survival hit the headlines. Rescue parties collected the three men on the other side of South Georgia. The twenty-two stranded on Elephant Island were all found alive.

In one of the most incredible stories ever told, all twenty-eight who set off on the *Endurance* in 1914 survived and were able to give their accounts of this unbelievable miracle. What shocked Ernest Shackleton more than anything was learning that the war was still raging two years on after he had left Britain, a conflict that he soon signed up to help with as soon as he returned to England in May 1917.

Despite all he had gone through, Shackleton returned to the Antarctic ice on a new expedition aboard the *Quest* in 1921. He got as far as South Georgia in January the following year when he became increasingly unwell. On 5 January 1922, he suffered a fatal heart attack and was buried on South Georgia near the whaling station that had saved him five years before. So ended the extraordinary life of an extremely adventurous man. His grave is today visited by tourists who come to the island to pay their respects to the explorer who gave the world one of the greatest survival stories ever told.

As for his ship, the *Endurance* still remains lost to this day despite several expeditions over the years. It is fair to say that one day the timbers of one of the world's most famous exploration vessels might once again be seen by human eyes.

Chapter 10

Britannic, 1916

For around eighty years the sister ship to the infamous *Titanic* had been pretty much forgotten about, consistently overshadowed in regards to the drama, the death toll and the shock surrounding the loss of the *Titanic*. But the story of the *Britannic* is no less fascinating and it starts at exactly the same place – Belfast. There were rumours that the ship's original name was to be *Gigantic* but that has since proved to be false.

When the *Olympic* and the *Titanic* were launched and sailed, the plans were always in line for a third ship of the same class which was to be named *Britannic*. She would be just as large and, after the disaster of the *Titanic*, much safer than anything they had built before. Firstly, she would be fitted with large gantry-style lifeboat davits that could hold six boats at a time; all the lessons learned after the inquiries were over would be smoothed out when the *Britannic* was brought into service.

She was launched from the same slipway at Harland & Wolff shipyard on 26 February 1914 and went into her fitting-out stage nearby. But this is where the similarities between the sisters ended because it was here that it was realized that she would not be picking up wealthy passengers for transatlantic crossings – she would be going to war.

By the time she was ready for service in December 1915, the First World War had already been raging for well over a year, and with the sinking of the *Lusitania* it was imperative that these colossal liners should be put to good use while they still had them. So, the *Britannic* would enter service under the control of the British government as a hospital ship: her job would be to ferry the wounded back from the battlefields of Europe safely back to Britain to be nursed back to health.

On 23 December that year, the liner pulled away from her berth at Liverpool and headed to the Aegean Sea where her sister ship, the *Olympic*, and the Cunard liners *Mauritania* and *Aquitania* were already busy. She successfully brought back thousands of wounded on several journeys over the next eleven months and garnered a reputation for being a reliable and spacious vessel, much more stable than the smaller hospital ships on the same runs.

Under the command of Captain Charles Bartlett, the *Britannic*'s sixth voyage had her making a stop at Naples for coal and supplies before heading out to the Greek islands towards her final destination at Lemnos. On 21 November 1916, she was heading through the Kea Channel close to the island of Kea itself with 1,066 people on board when, at 0812 that morning, there was all of a sudden, a huge explosion up forward.

Not knowing what had happened, the shocked crew and medical workers rushed around to try and find out how serious the damage was but were met with the ship taking on water and going down by the bow. Although the watertight doors were closed, the portholes had been left open and as the front of the ship subsided in the water, the extra openings flooded the ship faster than they should have.

Taking on a list, the ship's lifeboats were lowered with as many people as possible. From where they were sitting it seemed that the ship was going down much faster than the *Titanic* had at a comparable stage. Captain Bartlett carried on navigating the ship in an attempt to run it aground and save everybody, but this decision would be in vain as it was obvious in a very short time that the liner was doomed.

With the ship rolling further over to starboard, the lifeboats became unusable, and with the increased momentum of the ship, it was found that this was pushing the bow further down and there was no way she could be grounded so far from land.

The huge ship began to roll further onto her side with her still-turning propellers emerging from the sea. It was at this point that two of the lifeboats were dragged into the churning sea and, in full view of the other boats, were chopped up in seconds along with all the occupants. Thirty people were killed, the only deaths in the entire sinking.

With the Kea Channel being so shallow, the bow of *Britannic* had already hit the seabed 400 feet down, the rest of the ship rolling over and sinking sideways. Before long, all that was left was wreckage and lifeboats.

It took just fifty-five minutes for the ship to sink yet what was performed was one of the most astounding evacuations in shipwreck history. If it wasn't for the wayward propellers there would have been no deaths at all. Ships from all around the vicinity picked up the survivors. The few who died were later buried on land. It later became apparent that the *Britannic* had struck a German mine laid by submarine *U-73* a month before; several other ships would fall victim to this field over time. This did not stop people believing that the ship had been sunk by a torpedo in a war crime; however, despite what people chose to believe, the evidence proved conclusively that it was definitely a mine.

The *Britannic* became the largest passenger ship ever sunk and the largest ship sunk in the First World War. Not that it was much consolation for nurse Violet Jessop and fireman Arthur John Priest who had both survived this and had previously survived the sinking of *Titanic* and the collision between the *Olympic* and the *Hawke* (Violet Jessop would later write a book about her experiences).

The wreck of the *Britannic* was found in 1975 by ocean explorer Jacques Cousteau, who reported that the wreck lay flat on her starboard side with a huge hole in her port side, evidence it seemed of an outward explosion. But when Dr Robert Ballard visited the wreck twenty years later using more modern technology, it proved that what he had in fact found was the crack in the bow where the vessel had hit the seabed and bent back as the weight of the ship still on the surface built up pressure until she came to rest.

Over the years since Ballard's expedition, there have been several high-profile expeditions to the wreck, overseen by the current owner Simon Mills who has become the most sought-after *Britannic* historian that there is. Each time divers reach the wreck they unlock new secrets, including the positions of the watertight doors (some were not closed properly) and the location of the mines.

On one expedition in 2009, diver Carl Spencer died after getting into difficulties on the wreck, a reminder that a ship at such depth is still as dangerous today as she has always been. Ten years later a second diver lost his life.

As the *Britannic* today sits surprisingly well preserved, she will continue to fascinate maritime historians who regard her as another *Titanic* but within the reach of divers. But this ship has its own incredible story and its own enthusiasts who are reaching out today to find out more about the short life of this tragic, and for many years forgotten, sister.

Chapter 11

Mendi, 1917

When you think of a forgotten shipwreck, you might think the reason behind the lack of knowledge is because of the amount of time that has passed since the event, like the *Mary Rose*, or perhaps it didn't make the headlines due to a death toll that didn't whet the appetite of press reporters. But the tale of the SS *Mendi* is one that had a horrific death toll and was both shocking and scandalous at the same time in the height of wartime Britain; it is one that has only recently been properly documented and the stories brought to light.

The *Mendi* started out in 1905 as a new passenger steamship for the Liverpool-based British & African Steam Navigation Company Ltd that took on the Elder Dempster Line as her managers in order to secure the Liverpool to Africa routes. At 370 feet long and weighing in at 4,230 gross tons, she was a reliable vessel and one that plied her route for several years until wartime issues took over her running and she was requisitioned in 1916 to carry troops.

While in Cape Town, she would be ferrying 823 members of the 5th Battalion of the South African Native Labour Corps to Britain and then onto France to help with the trench warfare. In the case of these workers, they would be used for digging, construction and various other manual labour jobs instead of actual fighting. Despite the efforts of such troops, they were never honoured with any medals for their work and were kept segregated like third-class citizens.

They voyage went without a hitch, like so many other journeys that the *Mendi* had undertaken in the last twelve years, and after a stopover at Lagos (Nigeria) and Plymouth (UK), she began the final leg of her trip up the English Channel escorted by a Royal Navy warship, HMS *Brisk*.

By the early morning of 21 February 1917, she was south of the Isle of Wight in thick fog and running with low-visibility lights. Nearby was the mail ship SS *Darro*, also with greatly reduced lighting and not alerting anybody to her presence by sounding her horn, going at full speed. The *Darro* was much larger than the *Mendi*, over 11,000 gross tons, three times the size of the passenger vessel.

At around 0500 that morning the bow of the *Darro* slammed into the starboard side of the *Mendi* and ripped a large hole in the side of the ship. Captain Stump of the *Darro* did not stop his ship; instead, once she had broken free of the *Mendi*, seemed to continue on her journey, leaving the passenger ship to sink in the fog.

While there had already been many deaths on board from the force of the collision, there were still hundreds left to fend for themselves and amazingly they were surprisingly calm despite the dangers they were now facing. As she rolled to one side and developed a heavy list, the lifeboats were rendered useless, which caused massive concern when it was suddenly realized that most of them couldn't actually swim.

Stories of heroism came to light of the white crew giving up their space in the lifeboats for the black soldiers, something that was unheard of in those days. HMS *Brisk* lowered her boats and rushed to rescue as many people as possible as the *Mendi* slowly listed further over and finally slipped beneath the waves, leaving hundreds of survivors in the water. Many more were trapped below decks: they never stood a chance.

By now, the bow-damaged *Darro* had stopped, but for reasons that are still unclear to this day, she stood by with her lifeboats still on board and did nothing at all. When all the *Mendi* survivors were accounted for, it was now apparent that 646 people had died in the sinking, leaving just 267 survivors. This was one of the most shocking sea disasters off the coast of Great Britain and one that got even more controversial.

An inquiry was set up to determine the cause of the disaster and sat for five days in Westminster where evidence was heard by witnesses: the conclusion was that the fault lay with Captain Stump of the *Darro*. They summed it up by finding him guilty of travelling 'at a dangerously high speed in thick fog, and of having failed to ensure that his ship emitted the necessary fog signals'.

So, what punishment does a captain get for killing over 600 people? He simply had his master's licence suspended for a year. Had this occurred a century later, he would have faced manslaughter charges and a prison sentence. In the fog of war, a disaster like this with such a shocking loss of life was nothing compared to the thousands being killed daily in the trenches.

The wreck of the *Mendi* was known about but was not positively identified until the 1970s. Since then she has been dived on by explorers and historians, her upright hull now lying broken up, exposing her boilers. At some point her bell bearing the name *Mendi* was taken and nobody knew where it had gone or who had taken it. This was until 2017, near the 100th anniversary of the sinking, when it was anonymously handed over to a BBC journalist where it was put on show for the centenary commemorations at Southampton's SeaCity Museum. Prime Minister Theresa May returned the bell during an official visit to South Africa the following year where it remains on display today.

In 2006 the dead of the black South Africans were finally recognized at the same level of commemoration as any other Commonwealth war dead and the troops are now rightly recognized for their vital work during the First World War and beyond. Memorials to the dead of the sunken *Mendi* are in Southampton's Hollybrook Cemetery, as well as several more in South Africa in the towns and villages where the victims came from.

The Nuffield Southampton Theatre featured the play *SS Mendi: Dancing the Death Drill* in 2018, which told the story of the African troops on the *Mendi* and the tragedy of a shipwreck and how it affected those who survived after losing their breadwinners. With so many victims and so very little responsibility for their loss, this is a lesson that we must be made aware of. More than ever it is important today to commemorate the work undertaken by these troops and to pay respects to those who died for a country that they were no part of, yet willingly boarded a ship to their deaths only to be forgotten about. Thankfully, we now know the true story of the loss of the SS *Mendi* and we can now pay tribute to those who were lost so far away from home when a negligent captain cost the lives of over 600 men.

Chapter 12

Carpathia, 1918

Few ships in history occupy the maritime disaster hall of fame, but for the Cunard Line steamship *Carpathia* it was an incident completely unconnected to her that led to the name going down into the history books and becoming a household name.

Launched in 1902 from the Swan Hunter yard in Newcastle upon Tyne, she made her maiden voyage from Liverpool to Boston in May 1903 and proved to be a reliable and popular ship by all who sailed on her. At 558 feet long and 64.5 feet wide, her single funnel towered over her main decks, making her somewhat majestic despite her being rather plain in design.

For the next nine years she undertook various voyages that were all uneventful. On one voyage from New York to Fiume, Austria-Hungary, everybody thought the trip was going to be as usual as the rest – or so they thought. The master was Captain Arthur Rostron, a 42-year-old mariner who had begun his career at sea at the age of 15. He had only been in charge of the ship for three months when, on Sunday, 14 April 1912, the *Carpathia* found herself mid-Atlantic surrounded by icebergs and bitterly cold weather.

Harold Cottam, a 21-year-old wireless telegraphist – the ship's only radio operator – was getting ready for bed soon after midnight. It was now early Monday morning and as he was getting undressed, he put the headset back on to listen in to traffic just before he got into bed. He listened in to some random traffic right up until he heard a clear signal from the newest ship in the White Star fleet – the *Titanic*. What he heard shocked him. The ship was sending out distress signals and at first Cottam asked for confirmation. When the full reality of what was being said hit him, he raced up to the bridge.

Unable to make the officer of the watch respond fast enough, he raced to Captain Rostron's cabin and woke him up himself. This point was covered in several reconstructions over the years, most notably in the 1958 film *A Night To Remember* where he bursts in to 'What the devil's going on … Haven't you learned to knock before you come in here?' being shouted at him.

When Rostron was told of the distress call from the *Titanic* saying she was sinking after striking an iceberg, he immediately turned his ship about, prepared the lifeboats, roused the galley staff and had the crew muster blankets and medical supplies. The liner was sinking around fifty-eight miles away and he was sure that this was going to be a huge rescue operation.

Sure enough, when the ship reached the reported position, the lifeboats were sighted one by one. The pathetic remains of the largest and most luxurious ship in the world was heart-breaking. After a very early morning start, by daybreak they were sure that all the survivors had been picked up – just 705 people had survived out of over 2,200 on board. No other ship picked up survivors although several remained on the scene including the Leyland liner *Californian* which had been closer than *Carpathia* but stuck in ice and her radio operator had already turned in for the night.

On the voyage back to New York, the press hounded the ship constantly, but a news blackout led to speculation for the next few days about what had gone on. Lists of survivors had been released along with basic details by the shipping companies and other radio stations that had taken details, but when the *Carpathia* entered New York on Thursday, 18 April, the crowds of onlookers were shocked at the scene that greeted them. Dropping off the recovered *Titanic* lifeboats at the White Star Line pier, she then went alongside the Cunard Pier 54 where thousands waited in anticipation. A long line of bedraggled *Titanic* survivors, some of them in borrowed clothes, most of them mourning the loss of a fellow traveller or loved one, departed the ship to a life that had now changed forever.

The crew of *Carpathia* were labelled heroes and Captain Rostron was honoured with a host of awards and recognitions, the rest of the crew all awarded a medal commemorating the rescue. Some of them would give evidence at the disaster inquiries on both sides of the Atlantic and then the ship faded back into her normal voyages once again as the start of the First World War took the world's attention.

Carpathia was used to ferry troops to Europe across the Atlantic, back and forth, and she very nearly survived the conflict unscathed. But on 17

July 1918, while westbound carrying 166 crew and only 57 passengers, she was in convoy when she was suddenly torpedoed by the German submarine *U-55*. A second torpedo penetrated the hull plates into the engine room and killed five crew and rendered her a cripple. The captain, William Prothero, signalled the convoy to escape, which duly fled, leaving only the patrol boats to rescue survivors.

Incredibly, apart from the five killed in the explosion, every one of the remaining 218 on board survived. The *Carpathia* meanwhile slowly sank into the Atlantic until there was nothing left of her except the flotsam of a once-grand vessel. For her famous crew they lived a long life and were hailed as heroes until the day they died. Arthur Rostron lived until the Second World War when he was taken ill with pneumonia and died in 1940. Harold Cottam, the wireless operator, lived until 1984, long enough to see him being played in several films. While the crew of this ship are now long gone, their legacy lives on.

But that wasn't the end of the *Carpathia* story. Decades passed with only the *Titanic* part of her life being made famous, but as more people found out about her eventual demise in the Atlantic, a few interested parties started making plans to search for her wreckage.

In 1999, Graham Jessop began a search, funded by author Clive Cussler, for the wreck of the *Carpathia* after his father Keith had found the wreck of the cruiser HMS *Edinburgh* and recovered £40 million of gold in the Barents Sea in 1982, so he too wanted to get into wreck hunting. The first search turned up another ship, *Isis*, which sank in 1936.

A year later Mike Fletcher led a second search. In May 2000 they located another wreck, but it took until September of that year to confirm that the *Carpathia* had eventually been found, upright on the seabed at a depth of around 500 feet.

Since her discovery there have been several diving expeditions which have recovered items from the wreck and now there is a renewed interest in this most famous of lost ships. Although there are no memorials specifically to this ship, the names of the five who died that day in her engine room are inscribed on the Merchant Navy Memorial at Tower Hill, London. Her life, loss and story are now so well known that she will always be remembered as the ship that saved over 700 lives on a freezing cold Atlantic night over a century ago.

Chapter 13

Egypt, 1922

Talk about any shipwreck and images of a broken ship loaded with treasure fills the imagination and dreams of precious stones and lost bullion awaken the romantic adventurer in one. Of all the wrecks worldwide, most of them at best contain nothing but coal, perhaps munitions and whatever cargo it was carrying. But there are a few shipwrecks that do conform to the treasure-laden stereotype, one of these being the ocean liner *Egypt*.

Launched in Greenock in 1897, the *Egypt* was a 7,912-gross-ton passenger ship that was 499 feet long and could carry around 500 passengers and 300 crew. She was owned by P&O and used on the route that ran from Britain to India, at the time a very important 'jewel in the crown' of the British Empire. She was one of five sister ships, the others being *Arabic*, *China*, *India* and *Persia*, all designed for long-distance journeys making their owners one of the most travelled and famous liner companies in the world.

After her fitting-out period, *Egypt* sailed on her maiden voyage in September 1897 to Bombay, followed by various trips around the world to Australia, Egypt and India before war broke out in 1914. Like many other ships of her size, the *Egypt* was requisitioned as a hospital ship and, like the *Britannic*, she was painted white with red crosses and green stripes across her hull giving clear identification of her role. During this time, she saw action in the Dardanelles campaign and continued her duties right up until summer 1919 when she was finally handed back to her owners to resume her passenger-carrying services.

On 19 May 1922, she departed Tilbury in Essex bound for Bombay via Marseille, France, with only 44 passengers but with a crew of 294, the rest of her passengers joining the ship in France where they would avoid the treacherous Bay of Biscay which was notorious for stormy weather. But it was not only passengers she would carry on the trip. In her hold was over

£1 million worth of gold and silver bullion as well as gold sovereigns, a vast amount back in 1922 and one that would later excite those wanting to make a lot of money from her loss.

On the morning of 20 May she encountered fog off the French coast, which slowed her down to some extent, but her voyage continued mostly on track, until the late evening when she was forced to stop when visibility was dangerously reduced. Out of the fog the bridge on the *Egypt* heard a ship's siren in the distance, indicating that there was another vessel somewhere nearby. They knew that around twenty miles away was the Armen Lighthouse, which meant that they were not far from the Brittany coast. The siren belonged to the 1,383-ton French steamship *Seine* which was on a voyage from La Pallice to Le Havre and which at first was believed to be on a reciprocal course to *Egypt*'s But just minutes later the bow of the *Seine* appeared out of the fog and slammed straight into the port side of the *Egypt* and ripped the liner open in a screech of metal. Due to the voyages through the ice-covered Scandinavian regions, the *Seine* had an ice-strengthened bow which caused fatal damage to the hull of the *Egypt*.

The *Egypt* immediately took on a violent list and water flooded in at an alarming rate. Her occupants raced to get off the ship, only a few boats managing to get away from the sinking ship before they couldn't be lowered any more. Anything that could float was thrown into the sea to provide a flotation device for those that were now forced to jump into the water.

Although a distress call was sent out and several ships raced to the scene, the liner had gone within the space of just twenty minutes. The *Seine* was still nearby and had begun to rescue the survivors, but a total of eighty-seven people lost their lives in this disaster – seventy-one crew, fifteen passengers and one other who succumbed to the traumatic experience later in hospital.

With the *Egypt* gone, there was now talk of a huge salvage operation needed to recover the vast amount of gold and silver from the strongroom of the liner and for this was needed the best diving technology available and the strongest team that could be found. But first the wreck had to be located which proved to be a bigger task than first thought. After eight years of searching it was eventually found upright by the salvage vessel

Artiglio which was the command centre of the Italian Society for Marine Recovery for this operation.

Lying in 360 feet of water, the *Egypt* wreck was quite easy to navigate around due to the fact she was sitting proud on the seabed and not at some obscure angle or upside down as many wrecks so often are. The *Artiglio* and later her replacement *Artiglio II* (after the first one had been sunk in an explosion) had on board an 'observation shell' which was like a diving bell on the end of a crane in which a diver would descend and use the viewing ports to look out and then exit to carry out any work.

The first issue was to blast away at the upper decks of the ship and peel them away until they had got to the strongroom. Once this had been achieved, a mechanical grab would bring up the gold and deposit it on the deck of the salvage ship. Although this seemed an easy task, the operation was to carry on for five years until 98 per cent of her treasure had been raised.

Today the wreck of this once-magnificent liner is still explored by technical divers and does appear in some dive magazines now and again. Her history is just as fascinating as much as a 1920s liner ever was, but it was the loss and recovery of so much gold and the press images of those bars being held up by the salvage crew that the *Egypt* is most famous for. With the sweetness of the treasure story, it may be that much harder to forget that she had taken so many people with her when she sank almost a century ago.

Chapter 14

Morro Castle, 1934

S ome shipwrecks have a fascinating and gripping history and, in some cases, their final voyage is one that is wracked with mystery and unanswered questions. But there are few mysteries of the sea that are as strange as that of the American ocean liner *Morro Castle*.

Named after the fortress that guards the entrance to Havana Bay in Cuba, she was owned by the Ward Line and built for the New York to Havana route in 1930. Despite the Great Depression hitting trade for many businesses, this ship and her sister, *Oriente*, were never out of work. For four years she had success after success and became well liked, particularly for people who wanted to drink legally after the Prohibition Act banned all alcohol in America.

On 5 September 1934, she departed Havana for her regular journey which usually took around two and a half days. By the following day she was parallel to the coast of the United States and was heading north and into a batch of bad weather which saw increasing cloud cover, rain and a strong wind. There was a total of 318 passengers and a crew of 231 on board, although many say that this does not account for hidden passengers – smuggled children and stowaways, refugees from Cuba seeking a new life in America.

The evening of 7 September should have been the last night at sea for those on board, but something happened that would send shockwaves across the ship. Captain Robert Willmott decided to miss dining at the usual captain's table and instead had his dinner delivered to his quarters. Not long after this he began complaining of stomach problems. When they checked on him soon after, he was dead. The doctor was called who examined the body, pronouncing the cause of death to the best of his ability as 'acute indigestion'. The job of commanding the ship passed to Chief Officer William Warms who was not quite as qualified or experienced as Willmott, but there was nobody else. The only good thing was that the voyage would soon be over and all he had to do was guide the *Morro Castle* safely into port. With the passengers now stunned by the death of their captain, the evening ball was cancelled and most people retired to their cabins.

But events now took a drastic turn for the voyage, when at 0250 the following morning, a fire was detected near the First Class writing room on B Deck while only eight miles from land. While the first firefighting attempts were being made by the crew, they were quickly becoming overwhelmed as the fire spread quickly from forward to aft, fanned by the strong winds that the ship was sailing into.

It didn't take long for the electrical cable on the ship to be burned through. Luckily the ship did manage to get a distress call off in time but by now the vessel was crippled and losing the ability to manoeuvre. The *Morro Castle* was now adrift just a few miles off the coast of New Jersey and had begun to glow in the dark.

By now passengers were heading to the lifeboats and it was soon obvious that many of them couldn't be launched as more of the upper deck was cut off by the flames and thick smoke. The boats that did manage to get off only managed to save a limited number of people; the rest had to jump for their lives and cling to anything that could float such as deckchairs and life rings. Some suffered serious injury and even death from the impact of hitting the sea with lifejackets on, breaking their necks or rendering them unconscious to be taken by the cold of the North Atlantic or drowning in the dark.

By now several ships had responded to the SOS call and raced to the scene, the survivors being picked up by the *Andrea F. Luckenbach*, *Monarch of Bermuda* and *City of Savannah* with several other vessels searching the sea for any that had drifted away from the scene.

The burning *Morro Castle* was now listing to starboard, and with smoke pouring out of every available area on the upper deck, she looked a complete wreck. An aircraft flew out and was able to point out survivors to the rescue ships to search further afield in a shorter time period. When morning broke the ship had been totally abandoned and was now an empty hulk.

For the next few hours, the ship drifted towards the beach at Asbury Park in New Jersey and by the afternoon she had beached in full view of thousands of people who had seen the drama unfolding right on their doorstep. The charred liner continued to burn for two days until finally she was just a shell resting on the beach, a distressing yet intriguing tourist attraction and one that made photos of the disaster front-page news around the world. As the full scale of the tragedy became apparent, the death toll was revealed as being 137 passengers and crew – although, as mentioned, this does not take into account the stowaways.

An investigation showed that the fire may have been started deliberately but all the evidence went in the flames and the mystery of the fire and that of the death of her captain have never been solved.

Chief Officer Warms along with the Chief Engineer Eban Abbott and Ward Line vice-president Henry Cabaud were indicted on charges of wilful negligence and convicted. They were sent to jail but were later released on appeal.

A final twist to the *Morro Castle* story was the heroic radio operator George Rogers who sent out the distress signal without being ordered to – just before the power failed. It was his decision-making that alerted the rescue ships and saved countless lives and the inquiry recognized his actions as being worthy of mention. However, he was later convicted of making an explosive device that had injured a police colleague when it detonated. After serving time in jail, he was released to serve his country in the Second World War. In 1953, he brutally beat his two neighbours to death and received a life sentence. Looking at the man's history shows a trail of destruction and death, but his death in 1954 left one unanswered question: was Rogers responsible for the fire on the *Morro Castle* and the previous death of her captain? Many people who have researched this tragedy think that he was. But unless some new evidence comes to light, the final mystery will most likely never be solved.

Chapter 15

Athenia, 1939

When Britain and Germany went to war for the second time in just over two decades, nobody had any idea just how soon the conflict would be felt, but on 3 September 1939, a U-boat attacked and sank the passenger liner *Athenia* just eight hours after the official declaration of war following the Nazi invasion of Poland. The speed of the attack shocked the world.

The *Athenia* was built in Glasgow and launched in 1922, commencing her new career travelling transatlantic the following year. Owned by the Anchor-Donaldson Line (later the Donaldson Atlantic Line), she was 526 feet long and 13,465 gross tons, able to carry around 1,000 passengers and over 300 crew.

On 1 September 1939, with serious talk of war in the air, and despite the dangers looming, the *Athenia* departed the port of Glasgow and after a stopover in Belfast and Liverpool, she left England behind the following day and headed west towards Montreal in Canada with 1,103 passengers and 315 crew.

The following day, 3 September, the inevitable radio message from Prime Minister Neville Chamberlain announced that Britain was now at war with Nazi Germany, something that did not come as a huge shock, but was still terrible to hear. That evening the *Athenia* was steaming around sixty miles south of Rockall when the German submarine *U-30* sighted her and began tracking her course. Her commanding officer, Fritz-Julius Lemp, claimed that she looked to be doing a zigzag course and, due to the darkness, he figured she was possibly a troopship or armed merchant cruiser and therefore, in his eyes, a legitimate target.

At 1940 hours that evening, the *U-30* fired off at least two torpedoes, with one of them striking the liner on her port side and exploding on impact. The crippled ship immediately took on water and began to sink by the stern. A distress call was broadcast straight away and several ships responded and headed in her direction, including three Royal Navy warships that were in the area.

As the rescue ships pulled people out of the lifeboats and on board, a tragic incident occurred where one of the lifeboats got mangled by the propeller and killed its occupants in an accident that horrified those on board trying to save the already distressed survivors. A second lifeboat capsized the following morning in heavy seas, again killing several occupants. Throughout the night there were various incidents that caused death to the survivors as well as the injuries and icy-cold conditions that they were forced to endure.

For the *Athenia*, she was still afloat over fourteen hours later when she began her final plunge to the seabed. Going down stern first, her bow rose into the air until that too was gone. Although the various ships had rescued the survivors, they were going in opposite directions, so survivors ended up at either end of the Atlantic depending on where their rescue ship was heading.

The final death toll was ninety-eight passengers and nineteen crewmembers. But when it was revealed that the dead included fifty-four Canadians and twenty-eight Americans, Germany denied that they had sunk the liner, for fear that any admission of attacking a passenger liner on the high seas would draw those countries into the war on the side of the British, as it had done with the *Lusitania* in the previous war.

When the *U-30* arrived back in Germany, Lemp explained himself to the high command, saying he had been mistaken in attacking the ship and he thought she was armed at least. The coverup began by altering the submarine's log and brushing anything relating to the incident under the carpet. There would be no court martial or any more speak of what happened that night. Instead, they blamed the British for sinking it themselves in order to drag other countries into the war on their side, not than many people believed this.

It was only when the war was over and the Nuremberg Trials exposed a statement made by Admiral Dönitz admitting that the *U-30* had indeed sunk *Athenia* and that every effort had been made to cover this up and swearing everybody involved to absolute secrecy.

In 2006 the area where the ship went down was mapped by the Geological Survey of Ireland and the data gathered during that year interested many people, including wreck explorer David Mearns. He had gone on to find several wrecks of historic significance, such as HMS *Hood* and HMAS *Sydney* (see chapter on the *Derbyshire* for another one) and he took to scouring the data gathered for any sign of the wreck of the *Athenia*.

Sure enough, one Sonar contact fitted the bill and in 2017 he announced in his book *The Shipwreck Hunter* that he believed that the wreck of *Athenia* had been found and it was only a matter of time before he could launch an expedition to bring the first images back of the sunken remains. Upright on the seabed, her back broken, she is lying at a depth of 650 feet.

Today some of the names of those who died are engraved on the Merchant Navy sailors' memorial at Tower Hill in London and several more are dotted around Canada to commemorate her dead. Her sinking made the headlines as expected; with only hours passing since the war had begun, the death toll was already mounting out at sea. This was by far the most shocking start to any war, especially when she had sailed long before the declaration.

The tragic end of this liner heralded the beginning of six years of conflict where millions would die on land, sea and in the air. Although she was not forgotten, the first shipwreck of the war today still fascinates the reader, as we now wait for David Mearns to bring back those first images of the wreck of the *Athenia*.

Chapter 16

Admiral Graf Spee, 1939

As the Second World War entered its opening months, a number of German warships were already in position ready to strike at the heart of the enemy, for they had sailed months before war had been declared in anticipation of the future needs of the Reich. One of these ships was the 'pocket battleship' *Admiral Graf Spee* which was moving around the South Atlantic and Indian oceans in secret, ready for the order to strike at the enemy's merchant ships.

Launched in 1934, she was 610 feet long at just under 15,000 tons and was officially a Deutschland-class cruiser, her nickname 'pocket battleship' being given to her by the British due to her firepower resembling that of a smaller battleship.

After several years of patrols around Spain and some goodwill visits to various countries, she sailed from Wilhelmshaven on 21 August 1939 under the command of Captain Hans Langsdorff. When war was finally declared, the *Graf Spee* was already in position to commence sinking Allied merchant ships.

But Langsdorff was not like most captains. He would order the vessel to stop, allow all the crew to escape in the lifeboats, take on board some senior officers, and then sink the ship. After he had done this, he would transmit a distress message to ensure the crew would be picked up in the lifeboats before moving on to the next target. The information that the British had gained so far was that there was a raider of some kind in the area and for all merchant ships to be on the lookout. A fleet of Royal Navy ships headed out but they had a lot of ocean to cover and the enemy ship was operating in absolute secrecy and constantly moving areas.

Over the next three months, the *Graf Spee* sank nine ships, the searching warships baffled as to where she could be and frustrated that this was happening without any idea of where she was going to be next. But all that changed on 13 December 1939, off the coast of Uruguay, when three cruisers forming part of a task group sighted smoke on the horizon. HMS *Exeter*, HMS *Ajax* and HMNZS *Achilles* were led by Commodore Henry Harwood and the situation was suddenly changing in their favour.

Aboard the German ship, Langsdorff was convinced that a convoy was heading his way and decided to engage, but as they neared, he then realized that they were Royal Navy warships that had been dispatched to hunt him down. With the ships now closed up on their weapons, the *Graf Spee* opened fire on the *Exeter* at 0618 hours: the Battle of the River Plate had begun.

Over the next hour each ship registered hits; three smaller ships against one larger made it anyone's guess who would come out victorious. The *Graf Spee* took major damage and began to head towards the River Plate estuary. The *Exeter* had taken several major strikes that had killed sixty-one of her crew, *Achilles* had four dead and *Ajax* seven. *Graf Spee* had thirty-six killed and sixty more injured, all the while that her prisoners of war were locked below decks and unbeknown to the British that they were even there.

Exeter's damage was so bad that several of her main guns were out of action as well as the lines of communication which left the ship having to steer via sailors shouting in a line all the way from the bridge down to the engine room. But, incredibly, the one gun she did still have working fired a shot which landed right at the funnel of the *Graf Spee* and penetrated the vessel several decks down, leaving her fuel processing system destroyed. The German ship had no choice but to head to port as soon as possible as there was now no time to be able to head back home.

As the *Graf Spee* headed to the safety of the port of Montevideo, *Exeter* turned away in order to seek emergency repairs in the Falkland Islands, whence HMS *Cumberland* had recently departed in order to join the task force. *Ajax* and *Achilles* now waited at the entrance to the River Plate for the German ship to re-emerge from the neutral – but British-friendly – country and it was only a matter of time before the battle resumed.

Admiral Graf Spee anchored in Montevideo harbour and was finally safe, for the time being. But politics were now playing a dangerous game, for a ship such as this would not be allowed on neutral territory for more than twenty-four hours, although this could be extended due to damage. Another rule stated that a warship could not leave unless twenty-four hours had elapsed since the sailing of a ship under the flag of its adversary.

The sailing of merchant vessels was now secretly arranged, twenty-four hours apart, in order to keep the enemy ship in port so that more Royal Navy ships could get into position ready for the attack.

It was here that an incredible story of counter-intelligence was born. Careless talk cost lives, as the posters back in Britain said. You were to never talk about any military movements due to the fact that you never knew who was listening; spying was rife and intelligence-gathering worldwide was like a plague that you could not detect. People began talking over the phones, carelessly mentioning the fact that the aircraft carrier *Ark Royal* and the battlecruiser *Renown* were waiting off the River Plate, along with a host of other ships that were getting into position. This was bad news for the Germans who now only had a small amount of ammunition left for their heavily damaged ship. There was no way that they could sustain another battle, especially with the number of ships that were out in the roadstead. The forthcoming battle would be nothing more than a massacre.

Captain Hans Langsdorff knew exactly what to do when, after three days in harbour, he was ordered to leave. The *Graf Spee* weighed anchor and sailed on 18 December with only Langsdorff and forty men on board. When she was a short distance from the harbour, a tug took off the crew. With thousands watching the spectacle and with every man now at a safe distance, the warship exploded in a sheet of smoke and flames. The stunned public could not believe what they were watching. The *Graf Spee* slowly settled into the riverbed after burning for two days.

The fleet of warships waiting for the Germans was now found out to be non-existent. The *Ajax* and *Achilles*, both damaged in the battle, were the only ones there and it was possible that *Graf Spee* could have avoided them. Thanks to a clever bit of deception over the phones, the German navy had lost a major player. The scuttling of the *Graf Spee* made headlines around the world, but the captain never got over it. On 20 December, he locked himself in a Buenos Aires hotel and put a gun to his head in full uniform. Despite him officially being the enemy, even the British regarded him as a gentleman of war and an honourable man. The crews that he allowed to escape were rescued as were the prisoners of war, released when they arrived in Montevideo. The warships lying off the Plate turned for home and arrived back in Britain in triumph.

Today the wreck of the *Admiral Graf Spee* still lies where she sank; there have been several salvage missions over the years including finding her range finder and her huge eagle and swastika crest. Despite the sadness at the loss of so many lives and that of a proud warship, in the end Captain Hans Langsdorff made the right choice and for that he saved many more of his crew. To this day most people agree that Langsdorff's actions will always allow him to be labelled a hero, a title that he truly deserves.

Chapter 17

Bismarck, 1941

There are few episodes of maritime history packed with as much drama as the next shipwreck but this one deserves a special mention, because it has all the hallmarks of war, tragedy, passion and pride, all rolled into one. Never before had the world been gripped by the story of a ship as much as the chase that led to the end of Germany's greatest battleship and it is a story that is still retold to this day.

After the First World War, Germany was restricted in how large its military was allowed to be built up, and so when Hitler came to power, he knew that the first thing was to completely ignore any rules and order the largest armed forces that could be mustered. Part of this was the building of two huge battleships, the biggest the world had ever seen – the *Bismarck* and the *Tirpitz*.

These vessels would be over 800 feet long and over 50,000 tons fully loaded, with a complement of 2,000 crew to sail her. On 14 February 1939, the hull of the *Bismarck* was launched by Hitler himself at the Blohm & Voss shipyard in Hamburg and for the next two years she was fitted out and commenced sea trials around the Baltic with the shadow of the Second World War looming over her every move. With every part of the ship tested, she was finally ready to take on the role of the most powerful battleship which ever put to sea, and the Royal Navy had every reason to be concerned.

On 19 May 1941, she finally sailed from Gotenhafen (today Gdynia, Poland) and met up with the heavy cruiser *Prinz Eugen* on a mission called Operation Rheinubung, a sortie that was to see the two warships sneak out into the Atlantic Ocean and attack Allied convoys bringing vital supplies to an already struggling nation. All they needed to do was remain unseen.

But this failed at the first hurdle when a Swedish cruiser spotted her and 48 hours later, while anchored in a Norwegian fjord, an RAF Spitfire on a reconnaissance mission saw them both and took a photograph of them plain to see, which was immediately acted upon.

The Royal Navy dispatched ships from all around the Home Fleet to guard the entry points into the Atlantic from the areas that the *Bismarck* would be transiting. When another aircraft finally got through the bad weather to the same fjord, it was noted that the prey was no longer there and the two ships were heading out. The question was: which ships would come up against them?

On 23 May, two cruisers, HMS *Suffolk* and HMS *Norfolk*, sighted the two German ships and shadowed them, the larger vessels unable to shake them off. Messages giving updates were relayed to the Admiralty and two larger British warships were sent to intercept – the *Hood* and the *Prince of Wales*.

The battlecruiser HMS *Hood* was the largest ship in the Royal Navy, but by now she was over twenty years old, whereas HMS *Prince of Wales* was a new battleship, so new in fact she had still had contractors on board working on her systems, and who were forced to put to sea.

The following morning, 24 May 1941, the ships met for the first time and opened fire with their huge guns. Round after round hit both British ships and in one massive explosion the *Hood* was torn in half and sank in just a few minutes. The battle carried on a short while longer with the *Prince of Wales* before she had to withdraw with damage.

Of the *Hood's* complement of 1,418 sailors, only three survived. The sinking sent shockwaves not just around Britain, but around the world. A ship that had flown the flag for Britain during peacetime and had become one of the most loved ships ever known, was now gone forever. A furious Winston Churchill ordered the *Bismarck* to be sunk at all costs.

But hunting down a brand-new, powerful battleship was no easy task, especially when the best the British had had been sunk in minutes. The only thing they could do now was follow her and regroup, but the Germans had other ideas.

The next twenty-four hours saw more ships join the chase, including the aircraft carrier *Victorious*, but by now the *Prinz Eugen* had been detached from the *Bismarck's* side and ordered to carry on alone. In a moved that caught the British by surprise, the battleship increased speed and circled back on herself before they had the chance to track her, and then she disappeared from sight.

Bismarck had now successfully evaded her pursuers. After a damage report showed a light fuel leak after the engagement with the British, it was decided that she should head towards the French port of Brest which was under Nazi occupation. That way she could get repaired and refuelled before heading back out to continue the operation.

This whole time the Royal Navy was frantically searching the North Atlantic for *Bismarck* but were having no luck. It was only on the morning of 26 May that a Catalina flying boat from Coastal Command passed over the right area that at last the *Bismarck*'s position could be confirmed. By now she was too far away for the fleet to catch up with her, but the Royal Navy still had one more chance to catch her – the aircraft carrier HMS *Ark Royal*. In an incredible turn of events, an attack by a flimsy Swordfish biplane dropping a torpedo in the water was the answer, the resulting miraculous hit striking the stern of *Bismarck* and causing the rudder to jam while in the middle of a turn to port. The most powerful battleship in the world was now steaming round in circles.

On 27 May 1941, it seemed that the entire British fleet had descended on the area 600 miles west of Brest to close in on the *Bismarck*. That morning the battleships *King George V* and the *Rodney* pounded her with shellfire while the *Dorsetshire* fired torpedoes into the side of the armour plating. Fires erupted around the ship and it wasn't long before her guns were knocked out.

In less than two hours of battle the German battleship was a blazing wreck, and the order to abandon ship was given. Hundreds of sailors jumped into the water as the ship rolled over and sank, oil and wreckage on the water making swimming difficult, especially with the number of injured from the battle.

With two ships stopping to pick up survivors, word came about of a U-boat in the area and the rescue operation had to be abandoned. With eighty-five on board the *Dorsetshire* and twenty-five more on *Maori*, a further handful being later rescued by a trawler and a U-boat, the final survivor count was only 116 out of over 2,200 who were on board, with one of those succumbing to his injuries the day after the sinking.

The survivors were later taken to prisoner of war camps and saw out the rest of the war in Britain and Canada, but the story of the *Bismarck* does not end there. After his success with the discovery of the *Titanic*, Dr Robert Ballard had read about the story of the *Bismarck* and went

Mary Rose, salvaged after 437 years underwater. (*Mary Rose Trust*)

Mary Rose in her new museum today. (*Peter Kersten*)

Bonhomme Richard engages HMS *Serapis* at the Battle of Flamborough Head. (*Thomas Mitchell, 1735–90*)

The *Titanic* in Southampton for the start of her first and only voyage, 1912.

The wreck of the *Titanic*. (*NOAA*)

The *Empress of Ireland*.

The *Lusitania*, torpedoed off the southern coast of Ireland.

The *Endurance* in the Antarctic on her last expedition that propelled the expedition leader Ernest Shackleton into legend.

The *Britannic* as a hospital ship. She never carried her wealthy passengers; instead, she brought the wounded back home from the war.

The SS *Mendi* taken from a small boat. (*Debby Webster*)

The SS *Mendi* memorial at the University of Cape Town. (*Photo Axxter99/Wikimedia Commons*)

The *Carpathia* at Pier 54, New York.

The sinking of the *Carpathia*.

The *Morro Castle* burns off New Jersey after a number of mysterious incidents. (*C.V. Norris*)

The *Admiral Graf Spee* sinking off Montevideo. (*IWM/Royal Navy*)

The *Ark Royal* struggles to stay afloat after being torpedoed. (*IWM/Royal Navy*)

The *Normandie*. (*US Navy*)

The *Normandie* on fire at New York's Pier 88. (*US National Archives*)

HMS *Edinburgh* crippled and sinking with a cargo of gold bullion on board.

U-534 as a museum today. (*Author photo*)

The *Flying Enterprise* wallows and lists while salvors attempt to save her. (*US Navy photo*)

The *Princess Victoria*.

The *Andrea Doria* sinking after a collision with the liner *Stockholm*.

The *Andrea Doria* taking the final plunge to the seabed (Harry Trask, *Boston Evening Traveller*)

The *Edmund Fitzgerald.*

The *General Belgrano* sinking during the Falklands conflict after a torpedo attack by the submarine HMS *Conqueror.*

The *Doña Paz*.

The *Oceanos*. (*Peter J. Fitzpatrick*)

A life raft from the *Estonia* after the ferry sank in the Baltic with over 800 dead. (*Accident Investigation Board, Finland*)

The *Achille Lauro*. (*Les Chatfield*)

The *Achille Lauro* on fire and being evacuated. (*Mary Newlove Howland*)

The *Costa Concordia*, which sank at the island of Giglio. (*Roberto Vongher*)

searching for the wreck in 1988. After finding wreckage on the seabed that was later examined through photographs and found to be an old schooner, he returned a year later and hit the jackpot. For the first time in forty-eight years the world could see images of the wreck of the *Bismarck*. Her guns still pointed skywards, her main turrets had fallen out, her stern had broken off where the torpedo had most likely weakened the structure, and, most eerie of all, the paint had worn away on the deck to reveal the Nazi swastika which had been covered over as her first and last mission had begun.

Since the discovery there have been several more visits to the wreck and some astonishing images of this giant of the sea have been shown to the world. But the one image that brings home the complete waste of life in this case is the field of boots – some piled up, others lying side by side where a sailor had come to rest all those years ago. It is only then that we are humbled by the enormity of what we are seeing on our screens and remember that both *Bismarck* and *Hood* were full of people very much alike, serving their country at sea and paying the ultimate price in battle.

Chapter 18

HMS *Ark Royal*, 1941

Of all the warships ever made for the Royal Navy, one name soars above the rest for both celebrity status and infamy – *Ark Royal*. Aside from the original ship to bear that name in 1587, there have been four ships in the twentieth century to have had the honour of being called 'the Ark', each one of them aircraft carriers.

The third ship in history to bear the name was launched in 1937 at the Cammell Laird shipyard in Birkenhead, and displaced 22,000 tons when she was ready for service the following year. With a length of 800 feet, she could carry around sixty aircraft, mostly the Fairey Swordfish with foldable wings and the ability to deliver torpedo attacks against the enemy by simply dropping it from the undercarriage.

It was the outbreak of war that led to the original plan of the carrier deploying to the Far East to be re-evaluated: the *Ark Royal* was kept closer to home, being used between the Mediterranean and the Home Fleet depending on the situation at the time.

It was during her time serving with Force H in Gibraltar in 1941 that she had orders to head out into the Atlantic and help track down the *Bismarck*: the success of one of her Swordfish scoring a direct hit with a torpedo led to the battleship being cornered and sunk soon after.

The year 1941 was a busy one for the carrier: she was involved in many other campaigns including hunting the *Scharnhorst* and *Gneisenau*, as well as operations with the Malta convoys. With war springing up all across Europe, it was just a case of where best the ship could perform her duties; she was one of the most in-demand ships of the Second World War and, so far, she had performed with merit.

By November of that year she had returned to Gibraltar following more Malta operations; there was a warning of German U-boats operating in the area so it was vital to protect this floating airfield at all costs. Nearby was *U-81* that was waiting for the *Ark Royal* after intelligence suggested that Force H could be returning any time soon. On the afternoon of 13 November 1941, an explosion shook the midships section of the *Ark Royal* and killed one crewmember. *U-81* had fired a torpedo at the ship and struck her on the first attempt.

The *Ark* began to list straight away with the loss of half of her power following the failure of the starboard boiler room and switchboard. A huge hole in the ship was causing water to flood in and rock the ship further over, aircraft on her deck hanging on precariously while the escorting warships prepared to take on survivors.

Because of a loss of the internal communications, messages to stop the ship had to be relayed by word of mouth, and while the ship maintained its forward momentum, the hole was growing larger due to the forward motion, which ultimately doomed the ship.

Nearby, HMS *Legion* was moving alongside the carrier and started taking people off the ship; the rest of the crew mustered onto the flight deck to figure out who should stay on board and try and save the ship. While all this was being discussed, first-aid damage control was not being carried out and the ship was becoming more and more imperilled. Careless crewmembers leaving hatches open below decks allowed the flooding to increase at a faster rate, which soon reached the remaining areas of the engine and boiler rooms, causing a total loss of power.

There was nothing to do but try and get as many people off as possible. Incredibly, the ship appeared to stabilize and Admiral Somerville of Force H ordered damage-control parties back on board and attempt to save the ship. In all fairness, they did a good job and managed to restore some services and light one of the boilers, leading to fresh hope that the vessel could be saved. A tug out of Gibraltar managed to attach a towline, but by now she had started listing again and flooding more severely than before.

By the early hours of the following morning, it was time to leave the ship to her fate; it was a bitter blow, but the ship could not be saved. With everybody now evacuated, the ship listed further and further until she rolled completely over at 0619 hours and slipped beneath the waves.

Incredibly, the one able seaman who had died in the torpedo explosion was the only death on the ship; the time it took for her to sink gave everybody else a chance to get away, plus the presence of several vessels helped. All 1,487 survivors made for Gibraltar.

An inquiry was set up to establish the events surrounding the loss. The captain, Loben Maund, was court-martialled for negligence over the ship's state of readiness when it came to damage control and the evacuation. Although he was found guilty, the court did acknowledge that the welfare of his crew was his top priority. He would later become Director of Combined Operations and had a successful naval career, retiring as a rear admiral.

The *Ark Royal* was located in December 2002 during a search for the wreck as part of a BBC documentary on Royal Navy sea battles. When remotely operated vehicles with high-tech cameras were sent down, they brought back amazing images of the broken wreck and broadcast them to the world. She was found to be around eight miles from her last reported position and in two main pieces on the seabed. The stern section sits upright and the 66-foot-long bow section is upside down, separated by a large field of wreckage and debris.

Investigation of the wreck also found that the hull was under increased stress after the explosion and restarting her engines added to the flooding risk. Once power was lost to the ship, it became impossible to prevent the ship from sinking, a factor that was more a design issue than anything her captain could have done to prevent. With the ship now found, many questions can now be answered and the heroic actions of her crew honoured.

The name *Ark Royal* was later used on two more aircraft carriers, both of which have since been decommissioned and scrapped, but it is a name that lives on with pride, least of all through the memory of the most famous of the five *Arks* to have sailed the seas.

Chapter 19

USS *Arizona*, 1941

The 7 December 1941 will always be known as 'a date which will live in infamy' when the Japanese attacked the US Navy fleet and air bases at Pearl Harbor on the Hawaiian island of Oahu. The fallout of this major attack left the United States with no choice but to declare war on Japan the following day, to begin the campaign to defeat the enemy with Nazi Germany now in the mix. But the one ship that symbolizes the attack on Pearl Harbor is the USS *Arizona*, the vessel that had such a high death toll, and which accounts for around a third of the casualties that day.

That morning dawned like any other, a Sunday where the island could relax and be safe in the knowledge that the war that was sweeping the globe was far away. Anchored in Pearl Harbor that morning were several battleships, all lined up, each one of them carrying over a thousand crew and being honoured with the names of the states where they were affiliated – *West Virginia, Arizona, Tennessee, Utah, Oklahoma*. Several more were in the nearby dry docks and many more were dotted around, but the one thing that was missing was the US Navy fleet of aircraft carriers. It just so happened that the carriers had all left for various exercises and on that morning not one US carrier was to be seen. This proved to be a major blessing.

The USS *Arizona* was a fairly old battleship, certainly new ones were being built that would leave *Arizona* in the shadows, but she was still a good ship and her crew were well trained. She had recently been a film star when the movie *Here Comes the Navy* was filmed on board, starring James Cagney and a young Gloria Stewart (some might remember her as Old Rose in the 1997 film *Titanic*).

Launched in 1915, she was a Pennsylvania-class battleship at over 34,000 tons, was 608 feet long, and armed with twelve 14-inch guns on four turrets split forward and aft. In 1933 her crew had provided aid to survivors of an earthquake at Long Beach, California. Based there for most of her career, she had been moved to Pearl Harbor when the Japanese started escalating tensions in the Pacific arena.

Despite the confidence that the fighting was far away, things couldn't be further from the truth. Talks between America and Japan had broken down. A massive Japanese fleet of aircraft carriers and escorts had steamed undetected across the Pacific and was now in position just a few hundred miles from Oahu. As the dawn broke that sleepy Sunday morning, the aircraft took off from the Japanese carriers and headed towards Pearl. Their mission – surprise attack.

The first sign of trouble that morning was aircraft being picked up on RADAR. This was quickly dismissed as a squadron of US aircraft returning from a training mission. With no further warning of what was about to come, the Japanese planes swooped in low and dropped torpedoes on the affectionately known 'battleship row' and watched as one by one the resulting explosions shook the fleet.

The ratings in the harbour couldn't understand what was going on, but within minutes of watching the fleet being engulfed in flames and bombs being dropped onto the ships, they soon got themselves together and manned the guns up to fight back. Markings on the aircraft clearly identified them as Japanese.

It wasn't long before a large bomb was dropped by an aircraft and it slammed into the *Arizona*'s deck and penetrated deep into the ship. In just a couple of seconds the whole ship blew up and rose out of the water before fire and the pressure waves of the ammunition exploding ripped everything out of the ship and scattered it in every direction. With the shock of such a large ship being obliterated in such a short time, the sailors didn't have time to think about it, for the next aircraft were already inbound.

A second wave of fighters attacked the airfields and buildings nearby, leaving US fighters wrecked and nothing more than piles of burning scrap metal. Fuel and ammunition didn't have chance as one by one the depots exploded.

Back in the harbour the *West Virginia* had sunk, settled upright within the anchorage; the *Tennessee* suffered fatal damage but the most harrowing of all was the *Oklahoma*. After being hit by bombs and torpedoes she took on too much water to remain stable. The huge ship rolled over slowly until only her propellers and keel were visible. Rescue workers struggled to get people out of the ship, trapped as they were within the confines of the hull, but the ship was too tough to cut away.

After two waves of attacks, the Japanese planes withdrew. Because the US carriers were not there, Admiral Yamamoto decided to not launch a third wave. They would head home triumphant. They had lost only a handful of aircraft, shot down by lucky Americans who had manned the guns in time. But the Americans had lost an entire fleet, dozens of aircraft and nearly 3,000 people.

So why include the *Arizona* in this book when the attack took dozens of ships to their grave? Well, the incredible thing is that most of the ships were salvaged and nearly all were back in service to fight in the war. The *Oklahoma* was raised and towed away to be scrapped as she was too damaged to go back to sea, but she managed to sink mid-Pacific while on her way to the breaker's yard. The only two ships that weren't salvaged were the USS *Utah* and USS *Arizona*. While *Utah* is on the other side of the harbour and not as easy to access, the *Arizona* was singled out as the site for the official Pearl Harbor memorial.

As the war ended, plans were drawn up to have a permanent bridge built over the wreck across the middle, where visitors could gaze upon the wreck which sits just a few feet from the surface and every now and again releases a little patch of oil from somewhere inside. Rock 'n' Roll star Elvis Presley hosted a charity concert to raise the money for the memorial and it was officially opened in 1962. Today it lists all those who died in the attack on Pearl Harbor, especially the 1,177 who were lost on the USS *Arizona*. In front of the wrecked battleship is the USS *Missouri*, a ship that was built during wartime and proved successful during her long career; the *Missouri* was only retired in the 1990s, to become a museum. What is significant here is that the official surrender of the Japanese was signed aboard the *Missouri* in September 1945, exactly six years since Britain and France declared war on Germany. The two battleships now represent the beginning and the end of World War II for the United States of America, symbolizing both the tragedy and the victory.

Chapter 20

Normandie, 1942

One of the most magnificent ships to ever have sailed the seas and still live on through the hearts of her fans is the French liner, *Normandie*. The beauty of her interior and the graceful style of her hull made this unique ship extremely popular, least of all for her speed and class. The shape of her bow to look like a sailing tea clipper and the enclosed upper-deck areas made this modern-looking ship a marvel of the ocean and the pride of her owners, the French Line.

Built during the Great Depression, she was ordered from the Penhoet Shipyards after a large loan from the government to keep liners running to strengthen the French economy. Her design was such that speed became her major selling point; when she was launched and completed, there were high hopes for this magnificent seagoing palace, with all the best Art Deco designs incorporated within her passenger spaces right down to the advertisements announcing her maiden voyage. She was around 80,000 gross tons with a length of 1,029 feet, her three stumpy funnels giving her a sleek look about her: the builders certainly broke the mould when they built this!

On 29 May 1935, the *Normandie* met all her expectations and so much more when she broke all records and arrived in New York on 3 June, instantly winning the Blue Riband and very quickly becoming one of the most famous liners in the world, as well as the largest. The people who walked her decks and slept in her beds brought back tales of happy memories of a grand hotel combined with an opulent art palace.

For four years she sped across the Atlantic and the arrival of her closest rival, the British Cunard liner, the *Queen Mary*, set off a series of friendly competitions between the two which saw constant contests for the fastest liner.

But as with many ships, the sounds of war were looming and before long it was obvious that the fate of the *Normandie* would have to be decided.

The last thing anybody wanted to see was the grandest ship in the world flying the swastika flag. So, the decision was made to sail the liner to New York where she berthed at Pier 88 and where her fate would be decided.

As France fell to the Nazis, the powers that be realized that saving the *Normandie* had been a sound decision. The *Queen Mary* was already serving as a troopship; it was common to see the two ships berthed next to each other, *Normandie* still in the colours of the French Line, the *Queen Mary* sporting a new paint job of battleship grey and rust.

For over two years the ship remained at her pier until it was decided that she too would join her rival in transporting troops across the Atlantic. The *Queen Mary* alone had transported a record 15,000 personnel on just one transatlantic crossing (a record still held by her today, so with that in mind, work began on the *Normandie*. The first thing they did was rename her the USS *Lafayette* before the contractors came on board to start changing the most celebrated liner in the world to one of the largest personnel carriers in history. Fittings and luxury fixtures, artwork and statues were all ripped out in place of lifesaving equipment, bunks, stores and weapons stowage. With thousands of members of the armed forces about to make this their home, she had to be ready for war.

But in the haste to make her what she was never designed to do, the worst happened. On the afternoon of Monday, 9 February 1942, workmen were undertaking welding and cutting work in the First Class dining salon when suddenly a pile of life preservers caught fire, most likely from sparks flying around.

It was around 1530 hours that the fire quickly spread to the rest of the piled-up items left scattered around as the workers were forced to retreat from the room when the alarm was raised that the ship was now deemed to be on fire. At least 2,000 workmen were on board at the time and the race to get off the ship was chaotic. Over 200 were overcome by smoke and had to be treated as the ship was enveloped with toxic black smoke clouds.

Fire tugs raced to the scene as did emergency trucks on the jetty. Water was pumped from the River Hudson into the ship where they believed the seat of the fire was. By now the whole ship was billowing smoke from all her upper decks and had attracted sightseers for miles to see the ship burning alongside Pier 88 right on their doorstep. What worried some was the fact that the liner was beginning to list to port ever so slightly and this was gradually getting worse.

It took several hours to fight the fire but eventually the fire teams were successful; the smouldering staterooms and halls were now a wreck, but worse was yet to come as the amount of water pumped into the *Normandie* was now at a critical level and, without realizing it, the firefighters had seriously destabilized the ship. Unlike a land-based fire, there is nowhere for water to go in a ship other than down, so the ship simply listed that little bit further.

As the night wore on and into the next day the ship slowly and gently rolled over until the entire ship was on her side, like a sleeping giant, her rudder wedged under the pier, her funnels half buried in the muddy waters of the harbour. The sad sight that was now one of the most famous liners of the world was pitiful to see. Not only that but one of the workers who had jumped from a great height onto the pier later died, the sinking not being without its casualty in this case after all.

It would be a huge undertaking to remove the ship when it was obvious that she couldn't be repaired. After cutting away at her upper decks and funnels, the hull was slowly but surely worked on until she was gently righted by the United States Navy over the next year and a half, until, finally, she was upright again and fully pumped out on 15 September 1943, nineteen months after she had capsized.

A sorry state, the ship was then towed out of her berth for the first time in four years and sold for scrap, an inglorious end for such a glorious vessel.

Today the *Normandie* is still regarded as one, if not *the*, greatest liner that has ever sailed and certainly one that would have continued to be as popular long after her service had been completed in the Second World War. It is ironic that her final demise was caused by nothing more than a spark from a worker's torch and an unbelievably bad dose of hard luck.

Chapter 21

USS *Yorktown*, 1942

As the conflict between America and Japan intensified in the fight for control of the Pacific, both navies gave as good as they got when it came to each giving the other a hard time. The one type of vessel that was crucial to both sides was the aircraft carrier. Being so far away from their homelands, both the Japanese and US navies needed to protect their carriers at all times, for losing a carrier would surely lose the battle. One of these carriers was the USS *Yorktown* and she was about to take part in the most decisive battle of the entire Pacific war.

Launched by Eleanor Roosevelt, wife of President Franklin D. Roosevelt, she slid into the water for the first time on 4 April 1936 to the cheers of the builders who had spent the last two years working hard on her at the Newport News Shipbuilding yard in Virginia. In just eighteen months she was ready for sea and given the identification pennant number CV-5. Displacing 25,000 tons, she was 824 feet long overall, with an island towering above her starboard side ready to direct her ninety aircraft out and safely back again.

When war broke out in 1939, she found herself carrying out patrols in the Atlantic to protect the United States from attack by any German aggression: already US cargo ships and countless human lives were being lost, whether by accident or by deliberate targeting of convoys. Either way, the *Yorktown* joined three other carriers transiting up and down the East Coast, finally coming alongside Norfolk, Virginia, when the Pearl Harbor attack brought the country into the war with a sudden jolt.

The *Yorktown* was immediately dispatched to the Pacific and joined her sisters on the war front. Now she was doing this for real – there were no more patrols 'just in case', these enemies were real and the threat was very close. One of her first missions was to patrol the Coral Sea where, on 6 May 1942, during twilight hours three Japanese aircraft mistook *Yorktown* for their own carrier and attempted to land, only realizing their mistake when they were almost shot down. Three more made the same mistake soon after, with one being shot down.

Two days later the battle intensified when the carrier suffered bomb damage in an air attack. At the same time, the USS *Lexington* was damaged so severely and had to be scuttled. Losing a carrier was never a good sign but thankfully *Yorktown* could be repaired and she made for Pearl Harbor where she was put into dry dock. In just forty-eight hours of working around the clock, she was ready once again to put to sea.

By now another battle was looming on the horizon – at a small atoll known as Midway due to its location in the Pacific Ocean. On 30 May 1942, the *Yorktown* sailed once again to intercept the Japanese fleet that intelligence indicated was gathering just off the islands.

On the morning of 4 June, working closely with the two US carriers *Hornet* and *Enterprise*, she sent up a squadron of aircraft to search for what they believed was four ships, all of them aircraft carriers – *Akagi*, *Kaga*, *Hiryu* and *Soryu*. But of the forty-one aircraft that took off for the mission, only six arrived back to *Enterprise* and *Yorktown*, with none returning to *Hornet*. This was a devastating blow to the carriers' first patrol, but, incredibly, the day would turn around just as quickly.

Other aircraft from *Yorktown* and *Enterprise* found three of the Japanese carriers while their aircraft were still in the air and in an incredible stroke of luck, the Japanese were preparing the decks ready for the next mission and for the others to return. Fuelling stations had been set up on the flight decks and the others on deck were being re-armed right at the moment they were sighted.

The dive-bombers from *Yorktown* attacked *Soryu* while *Enterprise*'s aircraft concentrated on *Kaga* and *Akagi*, the bombs hitting the deck and causing massive explosions that devastated all three in just minutes. The fourth carrier, *Hiryu*, had broken away from her task force and launched her aircraft to search for the Americans, soon locating *Yorktown*. The Japanese aircraft attacked and scored several direct hits, which started fires and explosions throughout the ship; her boilers were shut down and she was now adrift in the middle of the Pacific but still afloat and still able to function. Incredibly, the crew below decks managed to get the ship moving again. The carrier even managed to launch further aircraft to go after the Japanese. But late that afternoon, with hope of getting *Yorktown* battleworthy again, suddenly two huge explosions rocked the ship as she took two torpedo hits from a nearby submarine that had been tracking her and which couldn't believe its luck when the carrier stopped in the water. But the *Yorktown* was still not done yet, for she stayed afloat for another two days. In the meantime, the remaining Japanese carrier *Hiryu* had been hit and sunk by *Yorktown*'s aircraft and joined the other three on the seabed.

The destroyer USS *Hammann* came alongside the *Yorktown* to assist with the pumping operations and damage control and became the command centre for her captain who by now was coordinating the saving of his ship from there with every confidence that she could survive.

But the *I-168* was in the area and the sight of an aircraft carrier and destroyer next to each other was too tempting a target to pass off. Remaining undetected and getting into a good firing position, she fired off four torpedoes. One hit the *Hammann* and immediately broke her back, sinking her instantly. Two others slammed into the already crippled *Yorktown* and the fourth missed completely.

By now the survivors of the *Hammann* were being rescued by the rest of the task group as were the *Yorktown* crew that had now abandoned any attempt at salvage. In the early hours of 7 June 1942, she took on a massively increasing list to port and rolled over. She slipped beneath the waves at 0701 that morning, with 141 of her crew going down with her.

The Battle of Midway was a turning point for the war in the Pacific. It was the first major defeat for the Japanese with the sinking of all four carriers of their task group, the Americans losing one carrier and one destroyer. In all, over 3,000 people were killed in those few days, most of them on the Japanese ships, with around 400 aircraft lost on both sides.

The wreck of the USS *Yorktown* was lost until 1998 when ocean explorer Dr Robert Ballard launched an expedition to search for the lost wrecks of Midway. In the research vessel *Laney Chouest*, Ballard used unmanned vehicles to search for the lost ships where a twenty-four-hour daily watch could continue to search so that no amount of time was wasted. With National Geographic filming the expedition thanks to Ballard's reputation for finding great shipwrecks, the mapping of the seabed began. They soon came upon a target that looked promising.

When cameras were lowered to the seabed three miles down, it was immediately obvious that, on 19 May 1998, they were looking at the first images of the wreck of the *Yorktown*. Upright on the seabed with a list to starboard, her decks and island appeared to be intact, almost looking like she was ready for battle again, fifty-six years after she had been abandoned.

Another expedition, this time financed by the late billionaire Paul Allen, set off in 2019 and successfully located the *Akagi* and *Kaga* within days of each other. As battlefields go, this was incredible to witness, but with three ships still awaiting discovery, it is anyone's guess when we will see them again, as only time will tell.

Chapter 22

HMS *Edinburgh*, 1942

O ne of the most terrifying aspects of the war at sea was the campaign known as the Arctic Convoys, a battle against both a physical enemy and that of Mother Nature in all her fury. The gruesome journey across the top of the world to and from the Russian ports was one of the most dangerous trips of the war, and each one was a gamble. One of the warships that was assigned to Arctic Convoy duties was the light cruiser HMS *Edinburgh*.

Launched in 1936 as one of ten Town-class cruisers, these ships were split into three sub-classes, in this case the Edinburgh class which consisted of just her and the *Belfast*. Displacing 13,175 tons, *Edinburgh* was 613.6 feet long and carried a complement of around 750 crew. Her twelve 6-inch guns on four main turrets were her main armament, which together with her smaller-calibre weapons, made this ship perfect for her role.

She was built in Newcastle at the Swan Hunter shipyard and commissioned into the Royal Navy on 6 July 1939, just two months before war was declared.

Her first attachment was to join the Home Fleet at Scapa Flow before moving on to other duties. She suffered slight damage during an air attack when a bombing raid on the naval base at Rosyth caught her but nothing too major.

The next few months would have her on a host of missions that made headlines, including the search for the *Scharnhorst* off Norway after the sinking of the armed merchant cruiser *Rawalpindi*, and also taking part in hunting down the *Bismarck* in mid-Atlantic before taking on further duties escorting convoys into the Mediterranean.

In December 1941 she was retasked to provide cover for the Arctic Convoys going to and from the Soviet Union where she was instrumental in ensuring these vital supply ships got through safely into friendly territory.

On 28 April 1942, the *Edinburgh* was the flagship of Rear Admiral Stuart Bonham-Carter, who was in charge of escorting Convoy QP 11 from Murmansk, seventeen ships about to head back into treacherous conditions that would endure for days. Nearby was the German submarine *U-456* under the command of Kapitänleutnant Max-Martin Teichert, who had been provided intelligence that a convoy was in the area; now all he had to do was wait and see when it appeared. On 30 April, the convoy came into sight and Teichert made his weapons ready.

When he was satisfied that he was aiming for the cruiser, he fired one torpedo which slammed into the *Edinburgh* on her starboard side, causing immediate internal damage and flooding. Thanks to the quick reactions of the crew closing watertight doors, the ship didn't sink; she was flooding but not in mortal danger just yet. Seeing this, *U-456* fired a second torpedo which devastated the cruiser's stern area, destroying her steering and giving the cruiser no way of proceeding on her own.

Incredibly, she was still not sinking; in fact, she was then taken in tow by the destroyers *Foresight* and *Forester*, along with four minesweepers escorting her. Despite constantly coming under attack by both air and sea, she lasted until 2 May when she even put up a brave fight against a German destroyer attack: she opened fire on one of the attacking ships that had to be scuttled due to the damage suffered. Even though she was a cripple herself, the *Edinburgh* was not done yet.

But it was later on that day that a torpedo meant for another ship struck her amidships and by this time she had taken on too much damage to safely return to Murmansk. It was with a heavy heart that the *Edinburgh* was finally abandoned and deliberately sunk by one last torpedo, from the *Foresight*, after her crew were rescued and other methods had failed.

In most cases the loss of a warship at the top of the world would be consigned to the history books, but in this case the *Edinburgh* had a secret buried within her hull that made researchers very interested in her long after the war had ended. What was kept quiet at the time was the fact that the ship carried a very valuable cargo – solid gold bars destined for the UK from the USSR as payment for war materials and military equipment. These were located in a strongroom almost exactly where the first U-boat torpedo had struck.

The British government was anxious to have the gold recovered quickly in case it was dived on and looted, and so salvage contracts were offered to several companies but none was up to the task for a variety of reasons, least of all it being close to a Soviet base in the middle of what was now the Cold War. But then along came Yorkshireman Keith Jessop who applied for and was granted the rights to recover the gold from the wreck and bring it to the surface.

By April 1981, the gold was worth around £40 million. The search for the wreck began using the research vessel *Dammtor*. Incredibly, the wreck was found in just two days and a robotic camera brought back confirmation that the cruiser had been located and identified on the seabed.

With the clock ticking, Jessop immediately got together a second expedition with the dive support ship *Stephaniturm* and headed out to the wreck. Using clearance divers, they descended to the 800-foot depth and cut away at the wreckage: usefully, the torpedo damage provided a way into the wreck but it still took a week to get to the right spot.

On 16 September the first gold bar was located and brought to the surface to the sounds of cheering as Jessop held the treasure above his head in triumph. The next couple of weeks were spent slowly bringing the ingots to the surface until the weather stopped all salvage operations, but by that time they had raised 431 out of 465 gold bars which meant that this operation had been a resounding success.

As the *Stephaniturm* departed the site, a memorial ceremony was held to remember all those who died in the sinking. A later expedition would recover twenty-nine bars, leaving just five still on the wreck, not worth diving for in the long run, and therefore leaving the *Edinburgh* to finally rest in peace.

The glint of gold does bring out every man and his dog to want a piece of the action and one of the losers in this case was Keith Jessop. After everybody had taken their cut and the gold had been divided up, Jessop was later accused of conspiring to defraud the unsuccessful bidders of the salvage contracts. He and a member of the Salvage Association were acquitted on all charges but his reputation never recovered. After working on other shipwrecks, including the silver-laden *John Barry* off Oman, he died in 2010 aged 77.

As for the *Edinburgh*, she rests on her side at the bottom of the Barents Sea, her gold story taking her into the realms of shipwreck legend. Her sister ship, HMS *Belfast*, is today berthed on the River Thames near Tower Bridge, the final survivor of the Town-class cruisers, as close as you can get to the *Edinburgh* and a great honour to all those who served on board both ships during those dreaded Arctic Convoys.

Chapter 23

Musashi, 1944

In the midst of the Second World War there were several warships that would come and go to claim the title of 'world's biggest warship' and the sister ships *Yamato* and *Musashi* were amongst them. Originally meant to be three Yamato-class super battleships, this was altered to two when the third hull was halted and eventually launched as an aircraft carrier. But both remaining ships had short but incredibly complex lives. We will visit *Yamato* in a later chapter, but for now we will concentrate on the behemoth that was the *Musashi*.

Designed in the 1930s, she was 862 feet long overall and displaced around 72,000 tons. With powerful engines she could speed through the water at 27 knots and her nine 18-inch guns on three turrets (two forward, one aft) could stand up to anything another battleship could throw at her. Advanced with the latest technology, she had the best sensors money could buy for early warning detection and a hangar below decks held up to seven aircraft which could be launched via a catapult on her stern.

Construction of *Musashi* began at the Mitsubishi shipyard in Nagasaki. On 1 November 1940, she was launched in absolute secrecy; the entire city was ordered to stay indoors for an 'attack drill' whereby an alarm would sound and residents would have to stay in their homes, never suspecting that just across the water the largest warship in the world was now afloat and being towed to a fitting-out basin. Being built behind a curtain of hemp rope for the last few years, the locals had no idea what was going on right on their doorstep.

In August 1942, she was commissioned into the Imperial Japanese Navy and by January was assigned to the Combined Fleet, which was led by the brilliant Admiral Isoroku Yamamoto. By the following month she had replaced her sister ship as the flagship and after the death of the admiral in his aircraft, shot down by an American plane in the Solomon Islands, his cremated remains were placed in his cabin on *Musashi*.

Over the next two years she carried out patrols but never really saw any action until 29 March 1944, when an American submarine found her and attacked by firing six torpedoes at her. Incredibly, only one hit the ship, causing damage near the bow which killed seven of her crew. After heading back to Kure Naval Arsenal for repairs, the navy took the opportunity to have her fitted with updated sensors and weapons systems before dispatching the ship back out into the Pacific once again. Her mission this time was to counterattack the American landings at Leyte.

When *Musashi* arrived with her task force at Leyte Gulf, carnage ensued before she had even seen an enemy ship, with several Imperial ships being torpedoed and sunk. On 24 October 1944 it was *Musashi*'s turn to be the target when she was attacked by torpedoes from US aircraft and suffered a large amount of damage. Just over an hour later, she was once again attacked from the air by bombs, one of which penetrated her upper decks and detonated near one of the engine rooms. By now things were starting to get serious as *Musashi* was already suffering from fires and flooding, but it still wasn't over, it seemed.

As the crew fought to stabilize the ship and repair the damage, power began failing and, that afternoon, with the ship's damage-control teams still fighting the previous incidents, the ship came under yet another air attack, this time from twenty-nine aircraft from the USS *Essex* and USS *Lexington*. Explosions rocked the ship as both bombs and torpedoes slammed into her, igniting fires all about and allowing more water to flood into the lower decks. It seemed that no amount of avoidance tactics made any difference: there were just too many bombs to avoid. By now the ship had a tremendous list and it was soon apparent that she could not take any more strikes.

But even as they fought to contain the damage, a further attack by another thirty-seven aircraft rained down on her with thirteen further bomb hits and an incredible eleven torpedoes striking the ship. By the time the attack had ended, she had been struck by an estimated nineteen torpedoes and seventeen bombs; at this point it was a miracle that the ship was still afloat, yet she somehow managed to limp away from the scene of the battle.

The captain attempted to correct the listing by flooding other compartments but this did not seem to work; the bow was now very low in the water and her list was only getting worse as the afternoon turned into evening. As all hope of saving her failed, she finally took on more water and rolled over. She sank at 1936 hours that evening, taking with her a total of 1,023 from her complement of 2,399 crew. The exhausted survivors were taken on board the nearby warships, with many of them being sent back to war more or less straight away.

Although it was marked on a chart where *Musashi* went down, she was not seen again until a team sponsored by Microsoft cofounder Paul Allen launched an expedition to hunt down the wreck using state-of-the-art technology on board the yacht *Octopus*. It took eight years of searching and painstaking research, but in March 2015 they proudly announced that the search for the *Musashi* was over.

Sitting at around 3,000 feet (almost a kilometre) beneath the surface, the wreck lay in several pieces with debris scattered among the larger sections. It is thought that she exploded after submerging, the cameras from the ROV's showing images of twisted wreckage and the terrible damage caused by the numerous attacks on her during that final day of battle. Ghostly images of the broken hull and gun barbettes allowed the search teams to make positive identification of the areas of interest and bring back amazing footage of this once-lost wreck.

The one poignant image was at the very tip of the bow where the seal of the Imperial Japanese Navy was once mounted, an empty space today giving us only a glimpse of what this mighty ship once was.

Chapter 24

Tirpitz, 1944

At the northern edge of the Norwegian fjords is the small town of Tromso, a peaceful setting for what was once the scene of the final battle to save one of Germany's most powerful battleships. Near the island of Hakoya is a lonely road with few houses, but if you know where to stop, you will be able to look and see huge craters dotted around the edge of the fields that lead onto the rocky beach. Look closer and you will find a monument made from the steel of the *Tirpitz*, a memorial to almost a thousand men who were to die here in a ship that never actually took part in anything like the headline-hitting fortnight her sister had been made famous for three years before. But it is the actions of her enemy that make this story fascinating.

After the launch of the *Bismarck*, *Tirpitz* soon followed less than two months later, on 1 April 1939, at Wilhelmshaven, and was commissioned into the fleet on 25 February 1941 after conducting her trials for the first time. But with *Bismarck* sunk in the May, it was imperative that *Tirpitz* be protected at all costs – even when she was being built, bombing raids had slowed work despite the ship not taking any actual hits.

In early 1942 the battleship was deployed to Norway with every intention of attacking Allied convoys but, alas, fuel shortages were so bad that the *Tirpitz* never seemed to do anything significant and was soon nicknamed the 'Lonely Queen of the North' by some. British air attacks continued at every opportunity, without success, but while the ship was being shuffled around the fjords, brilliant thinkers were getting together in the UK to devise a bold and audacious plan to sink the *Tirpitz*.

Operation Source was put into action in September 1943 after almost a year in the planning. Midget three-man submarines would be towed from a base in Scotland and released off Norway, to then slowly make their way through to the *Tirpitz*'s berth in Kaafjord, cut through anti-submarine netting and release explosive charges specially shaped to fit around both sides of the submarines. The explosives placed under the hull should cause enough damage to sink her. On 22 September, the three submarines, *X5*, *X6* and *X7*, approached *Tirpitz* and two out of the three managed to lay their charges before the battleship's crew was alerted to an attack taking place.

X6 and *X7* were captured and their crews brought aboard, the submarines abandoned and left to sink. With only an hour to go before the detonation, the captives informed their German captors what they had done. There was little time to do anything and the subsequent blasts ripped holes in the hull, causing extensive damage. (Nobody had seen *X5* since the attack began and searches for the wreck and her crew of three have since drawn a blank.)

After having major repairs carried out where she stood, it was decided to move the *Tirpitz* once again but not before a significant bombing attack on 3 April 1944 killed well over 100 of her crew – reports differ on the exact total – and seriously damaged her in several places.

Over the next few months, the ship endured more and more air raids; the British were determined to sink the *Tirpitz*, but she seemed almost indestructible. By 29 October, she had already moved away to Hakoya Island near Tromso, but the bombing raids kept on coming. She had so much damage that couldn't be repaired but she was still at fighting capability even though there was very little chance of her leaving port what with the fuel shortages.

On 12 November 1944, the RAF launched the most devastating raid yet on the *Tirpitz* when thirty-two Lancaster bombers were dispatched from 9 and 617 Squadrons. On board each of these was a bomb designated Tallboy, another design by Barnes Wallis who had given 617 Squadron the famous 'bouncing bomb' for the 'Dambusters' raid the year before.

The *Tirpitz* was anchored next to sandbank to prevent her from capsizing if hit, but the Tallboy explosions blew that away, as well as causing serious damage to the ship itself even though she had sustained just three direct hits. In all, twenty-nine Tallboys were dropped, which destroyed the submarine netting, shifted the sandbank and left huge craters in the surrounding beach area and grassland. Large holes in the hull were letting in water and the ship began to list heavily until finally the order to abandon ship was given. A massive explosion sent Turret Caesar (the second turret from the stern) flying into the air, landing on survivors swimming away. After so many raids, the *Tirpitz* finally rolled over at 0950 that morning, her propellers sticking into the air.

As with anything during this time, there is confusion over how many people actually died; the likelihood is that around 950 were lost, a devastating toll considering the role she actually played in the war.

After the war, with the wreck of the *Tirpitz* lying so close to land, upside down, a Norwegian man bought the wreck for scrap metal and began cutting her up piece by piece. From 1948, he had a team of salvors working hard taking the ship apart: considering her armour and why she was built, this was a lot of scrap metal to be had. In the nine years it took him, he successfully took the ship to pieces and had made a lot of money on the sale.

What is interesting here is that the pieces that couldn't be sold for scrap were taken as souvenirs by the salvage teams. These artefacts remained with them for decades and were probably passed down through the families until a Second World War bunker in Tromso was converted into a museum dedicated to the *Tirpitz*. An appeal was put out for anybody who had such items to come forward.

So many people did that the museum is now full of amazing *Tirpitz* relics that tell the visitor the story of the battleship and the final raid that ended her career. From a wall clock to a life raft, these items are today on display, along with the memories of those who sailed on her, sunk her and eventually salvaged her.

Standing at the site of the bombing raid on Hakoya, it is odd to think that this quiet beach with very few people living nearby could have been the scene of so many deaths on one of the most famous air raids of the Second World War. Here and there the beach still shows signs of the *Tirpitz*, with a gun mounting lying rusty and abandoned or a random chain leading out into the sea. But with museums like the one in the bunker and the people who run them, the story of the *Tirpitz* will never be forgotten and neither will her lost crew.

Chapter 25

Wilhelm Gustloff, 1945

O f all the shipwrecks in the world, there are very few that can be
considered the worst regarding death tolls, but the sinking of
the *Wilhelm Gustloff* is the one ship that has taken more lives
than any other and remains to this day officially the worst sea disaster in
history.

But she started out as a ship designed for pleasure and holidays through
a programme known as Strength Through Joy, giving the working
people of Nazi Germany the relaxation needed in order to get maximum
cooperation when it was time to work. This was a public relations victory
as holiday camps and concerts joined the list of things that the working
German could look forward to under the pretence of helping make
Germany a world leader.

Named after an assassinated Nazi leader, the *Wilhelm Gustloff* was
launched at the Blohm & Voss shipyard in Hamburg on 5 May 1937,
being 684 feet long and 25,484 gross tons. Her white hull and single
funnel, as well as the style of lettering on the bow, made this ship unique
and, it was hoped, the first of many such liners.

Her career was a short one when it came to doing what she was meant
to do: before her maiden voyage even had the chance to begin, she found
herself assisting with the rescue of the cargo ship *Pegaway* during a storm
in the North Sea on 4 April 1938. The ship eventually sank and her crew
were taken aboard the liner. The maiden voyage was also not without
incident when on day two of the cruise her captain had a heart attack on
the bridge and died. The man who replaced him was Friedrich Petersen
who would finish the voyage and then command it one more time, on her
final voyage.

When war broke out, she was re-tasked as a hospital ship before being
painted grey and later serving as an accommodation ship in Gotenhafen
(now Gdynia). Here she would stay for some four years before being

used as a transport ship for what was now looking like an evacuation of German people from areas under threat of invasion by Soviet troops in East Prussia and the Baltic states.

On the afternoon of 30 January 1945, the *Wilhelm Gustloff* was loaded up with over 10,500 people during the evacuation of Danzig (now Gdansk). She had on board her crew of 173 as well as various military personnel and around 9,000 civilian refugees, with every space below decks used up by refugees fleeing the Red Army. The heat and the humidity were unbearable, with many people stripping off their lifejackets despite being advised to keep them on. As the ship headed out into the Baltic Sea, she was forced to display her navigation lights due to a convoy being in the area, which made her not only easy to spot, but also the way the ship was painted left anybody watching in no doubt that she was not a hospital ship nor was she civilian: grey paint meant military vessel and the Soviet submarine *S-13* knew this when she sighted the liner later that night.

Tracking the ship for several hours, the submarine finally had her lined up in its sights. At around 2100 hours, Captain Alexander Marinesko ordered the firing of four torpedoes, one of which failed to fire. The remaining three slammed into the *Wilhelm Gustloff*'s port side which devastated the ship immediately. Heavy damage and flooding caused the ship to lose power as her engines were disabled, and it was obvious that the ship was immediately doomed.

With so many people on board, it proved impossible to get everybody onto the lifeboats and only nine could be used, the rest breaking free or being completely seized up. People started to panic as the ship lurched from side to side, the freezing temperatures outside not offering the passengers much hope of survival if they weren't rescued.

But after just forty minutes, the *Wilhelm Gustloff* had sunk below the waves. Thousands of people were floating around in the sea. Incredibly, despite the icy-cold sea (it was January after all), 996 people were pulled out of the water alive by several minesweepers and patrol vessels. But with so many trapped below decks, there were no more survivors to be found. (Other sources say around 1,200 survivors were rescued.)

The death toll in the sinking of this ship has been hotly debated by researchers for decades: it is anything between 9,343 and 9,600. Either way, no ship has ever come close to this and hopefully never will. This is a world record that nobody wants to break and with so many of the victims unidentified, many of them will never be known. Just days after she sank the *Wilhelm Gustloff*, the submarine *S-13* would go on to sink the *General von Steuben*, killing a further 4,500. Those last few months of the war would see several more sinkings like this and each one would be just as shocking.

The wreck of the *Wilhelm Gustloff* today lies on her port side, the midships section has collapsed in on itself with the bow and stern remaining mostly intact. She is officially a war grave and diving is not permitted on her without special permission. There have been rumours of the lost treasure known as the Amber Room being on board, which has led to treasure hunters wanting to search her for evidence, but so far nothing has been proved. Several items had previously been recovered from the wreckage and are now on display in various war and maritime museums in both Poland and Germany.

Despite the huge death toll, the sinking of the *Wilhelm Gustloff* was forgotten about for many years; few people had ever heard of it and even today her name is not one that rolls off the tongue. It is only with the publication of recent books and even the release of a film, that the world has become more knowledgeable about this wreck, and over time her victims will be remembered once more.

Chapter 26

Yamato, 1945

In the closing months of the Second World War, the Imperial Japanese Navy was making desperate attempts to regain a modicum of control of the Pacific following the turning point at Midway and the loss of so many of her capital ships.

The battleship *Yamato*, sister to *Musashi*, was the lead ship of the class and was launched on 8 August 1940 at the Kure Naval Arsenal where she was fitted out, and, by the look of her, covered in guns from stem to stern. At 839 feet 11 inches long, she was around 71,000 tons and looked identical to her sister in both style and armament. Work progressed well and she was actually commissioned into the fleet early and became Admiral Yamamoto's flagship for a year before her sister took over. Working closely with *Musashi*, the two ships were designated convoy escorts working out of Truk where at one point *Yamato* suffered torpedo damage from a submarine attack. She was sent to the Kure dry dock in January 1944 for repairs and temporary patching to prevent further flooding before she was once again ready to put to sea.

On 24 October 1944, she suffered bomb damage during the Battle of Leyte Gulf in the same sortie that led to the sinking of *Musashi*; she took on water but remained able to fight. She opened fire on the American ships and scored hits on the USS *Gambier Bay*, an escort carrier, that led to the *Yamato* having torpedoes sent her way. Luckily, she avoided them and the following month found herself once again under attack by a submarine where she sustained further damage that led to her again being placed in a dry dock for repairs and upgrades.

When American forces landed on Okinawa, *Yamato* was ordered to sail with the fleet to attack the vast US Navy assembly off Okinawa. But US radio intercepts had already anticipated this and the arrival of the Japanese ships came as no surprise to the Americans. All available forces were waiting for them, ready to engage, and on 7 April 1945, the two forces drew together.

It would be the early afternoon before any action took place with the sinking of a destroyer by US aircraft which then turned on the *Yamato* and the rest of the fleet. By now this was a full-scale air attack and the Japanese found themselves overwhelmed. The battleship found herself to be taking several hits simultaneously, her upper deck taking a pounding and fires erupting inside the compartments.

By now torpedoes had found their way to the *Yamato* and three struck her in the engine and boiler rooms, crippling the ship. Anti-aircraft fire proved useless as fuses were detonating prematurely. More torpedoes struck the ship as the sea gushed in, causing a list that could not be altered.

Yamato had started to lose power, with fires burning all over the ship and black smoke belching from the lower decks, while the bombs kept raining down, causing heavy loss of life. Like *Musashi* the year before, the crew tried to counter the list by flooding other compartments, but this was also in vain. In less than two hours the ship was doomed and the order was given to abandon ship. Growing concerns for the safety of the magazines were highlighted but they could not be flooded as the pumping stations had been disabled.

As the ship rolled to one side, more torpedoes struck the ship, only this time hitting the underside of the exposed hull. As the power failed completely, the crew jumped into the sea when suddenly the ship erupted in a massive explosion that sent a vast black cloud into the air hundreds of feet high. This was one of the forward magazines finally detonating its deadly contents and tearing the ship up into scrap metal.

By the time the smoke had cleared *Yamato* had gone, and with her 3,055 crew. Only 277 survivors were picked up by the other ships in the task group. The Battle of Okinawa was a victory for the Americans who remained on the island whence they continued the Pacific campaign until the end of hostilities.

The wreck of the *Yamato* was thought to have been found in 1982, but nothing could be confirmed for two years, only then after the first images of the wreck had been released. The explosion had torn the ship into two major sections and left a trail of mess in between. The bow section is upright with the crest of the Imperial Navy still visible on her tip, the stern completely upside down with her propellers now the only visible part of this end.

Several surveys of the wreck have been carried out over the years and there has been an increased interest in the wreck, especially with the discovery of other wrecks in the Pacific in recent years. Today the Kure Maritime Museum celebrates the life of the battleship and speaks volumes about her history, as well as having a huge model taking pride of place in the entrance hall. It is place to remember all those who went down with her in 1945 when the end of the war was just a few months away.

Chapter 27

U-534, 1945

The scourge of the U-boats began in the First World War when this new and unseen weapon wreaked havoc on the shipping convoys, all the more so after the sinking of the *Lusitania* proving that just one torpedo could sink such large vessels and kill so many people. When the Second World War broke out, the U-boat menace returned with a vengeance, only this time they were more modern and more deadly. Most of all – there were now hundreds of them!

As the Battle of the Atlantic was being won with the new sensor equipment, ASDIC and later SONAR, detecting the submarines which would then be sent a barrage of depth charges to sink them. Astonishingly, the tide turned and the hunters became the hunted. By the end of the war 784 U-boats had been sunk and destroyed out of 1,162 that had been built. The cost in lives lost exceeded 30,000.

Out of all the U-boats that went down in that period, there are so many with fascinating stories that it would be impossible to list them all. The ones that were captured with Enigma machines, the submarines that sank the great liners and the ones that were so brave that even they gained the admiration of the enemy they were trying to sink.

U-534 was launched on 23 September 1942 and was commissioned exactly three months later. Built in Hamburg, she was 251 feet long and displaced 1,257 tons submerged/1,144 tons surfaced. Her two shafts connecting to her two engines produced a reasonable 18 knots on the surface with around 7 knots submerged; her crew of forty-eight squeezed into the tiny spaces that was submarine life and would sometimes have to live like that for days if they were in a war zone.

Many of the U-boats would surface when the coast was clear: they needed fresh air and the opportunity to recharge the batteries as they couldn't run their diesel engines underwater as there was nowhere for the exhaust fumes to go unless they wanted to be spotted by the bubbles.

From May 1944, *U–534* worked with two other submarines conducting weather patrols off Greenland, but this was not to last long when she sustained oil leaks and ran into bad weather. During August she was attacked by an aircraft but suffered no damage, the same thing happening two days later before she managed to put into a French port.

After being fitted with a *schnorchel* (snorkel), the *U–534* put to sea again and used it for the first time, but the exhaust fumes entering the boat caused several crewmembers to collapse, and when she surfaced she was immediately attacked by a Wellington bomber, which the *U–534* promptly shot down.

By October she had arrived in Kiel and underwent a refit period until 1 May 1945, when the war was just days away from coming to an end. On 5 May, the commander of *U–534* was informed of the partial surrender by Admiral Dönitz and that a ceasefire was in effect south of the 56th parallel. With fifty-two crew on board, she sailed and headed north in order to form a convoy with other submarines, but instead she was spotted by two RAF Liberators off the island of Anholt, between Denmark and Sweden, and they swooped down to attack her.

The gun crews closed up and opened fire, shooting down one of the aircraft before she avoided a barrage of depth charges from the remaining Liberator. Another depth charge exploded close by and the boat began taking in water at the stern. She sank to the seabed where the crew began exiting and swimming to the surface. All crew managed to leave the *U–534* alive, but one died on the way to the surface due to lung damage (he failed to exhale on the way up) and two others died of exposure before they had a chance to be rescued.

The wreck was located in 1986 and, as the years went by, a rumour of hidden treasure reared its head, with stories of the submarine being filled with priceless objects that the Nazis didn't want to fall into the enemy's hands when Germany fell. The Dutch salvage company Smit Ltd took on the task of raising the submarine from a depth of sixty-seven metres which was sponsored by Karsten Ree, a Danish media millionaire. With the submarine attached to a crane barge, the lifting of the boat slowly began on 23 August 1993, with the excited salvage teams watching.

With cheers and the cameras rolling, the conning tower of *U–534* broke the surface for the first time in forty-eight years and she was once again heading towards dry land. Due to her three victims not being on board the submarine, she was never classed as a war grave, therefore didn't come under any protection. But it was soon found that the whole salvage operation was in vain when they found no Nazi treasure. Instead, they found some interesting items that could be preserved, such as binoculars, shoes, food tins, wine and thousands of condoms (to be filled with air and released with metal strips attached to confuse enemy RADAR).

With the disappointment evident, she was no longer useful to the salvage operation, and she was soon acquired by a group called the Warship Preservation Trust which brought the submarine on a barge over to Birkenhead in Merseyside, in May 1996, ironically the destination of many of her potential targets.

For several years she stood on display next to the Rothesay-class frigate HMS *Plymouth* and the submarine HMS *Onyx* before the museum ceased trading in 2006. With *Onyx* and *Plymouth* now scrapped, *U-534* thankfully had a saviour in the form of Merseytravel, who put forward plans to turn her into a permanent museum with all her artefacts on display. To get her to the new purpose-built site she was cut into five sections for transportation; when she arrived, two sections were re-joined but the rest were kept as they were, preserved with glass panels placed in front of the openings. This very unique museum – the U-boat Story Museum – now has the visitors viewing the internal workings of *U-534*, with diagrams and information boards providing a full rundown of what went on and what was found in each section. As it is something that has never been done before, it has really paid off and is a fascinating place to visit.

The museum opened on 10 February 2009 and has become one of Merseyside's best tourist attractions and the world's most unique museum, dedicated as it is to a U-boat. With so many submarines still missing, this is a fitting tribute to the sailors of the submarine service who faced hard times and tough conditions, many of them never returning home. With the full story of *U-534* now on show for all to see, we can now ensure that this story is kept alive, for all their sakes.

Chapter 28

Flying Enterprise, 1952

The press love a good rescue story, especially one that comes with a heart-warming and feel-good ending, but the drama that overtook the *Flying Enterprise* in the middle of the Atlantic ticked almost every box that media coverage could hope for.

The *Flying Enterprise* was a freighter built for the War Shipping Administration in California in 1944 as the *Cape Kumkaki*. She was renamed in 1947 when she changed owners to the Isbrandtsen Company for general cargo on the transatlantic routes. She was 396 feet 5 inches long, 6,711 gross tons and could travel at a reasonable speed of 14 knots while carrying forty-eight crew as well as up to ten passengers.

In the run-up to Christmas 1951, she was alongside Hamburg, Germany, loading up with a random cargo of pig iron, peat moss, coffee, Volkswagen cars and antiques. When her ten passengers were safely on board, the ship slipped anchor and put to sea on 21 December bound for New York. As she made her way through the English Channel, she encountered heavy fog but nothing to worry about.

In command was Henrik Kurt Carlsen, the 37-year-old captain who had spent his life since the age of 14 at sea, commanding his first ship at just 22. The sea was starting to pick up and rock the ship around a bit but this was nothing new to a man like Carlsen; he had encountered worse before and would most likely do so again.

Christmas Day came and went, the ship tossing and turning with every wave, but it was now becoming evident that the ship was entering hurricane-style weather, and two days later several loud bangs were heard coming from the hull itself. An inspection of the ship showed that she was starting to suffer structural damage in the form of two large cracks that ran down the hull from one side of the ship to the other. This was very worrying, especially since she was now taking a huge battering from the waves. Carlsen needed to put in to the nearest port as soon as possible, be that turning back to Britain or heading to the Azores.

On the morning of 28 December, the *Flying Enterprise* was rolling over by around 20 degrees each time, but then a huge wave sent her over up to 70 degrees to port. The dramatic change in momentum shifted the cargo; with the centre of gravity changing, the ship could not recover from such a roll. Although the ship tried to right itself, she now had a permanent list of around 25 degrees that she could not come back from. The engines were starting to fail due to the lubricating oil not being able to get to the parts, so Carlsen ordered an SOS sent out to all ships.

It would be around twenty-four hours before the closest ship could get to her when the cargo ship *Sherborne* and the US Navy transport vessel USS *General A. W. Greely* came to her aid. They started sending lifeboats over to rescue the passengers and crew but one male passenger died in the process, the rest of her complement taken safely aboard both ships. Now the only person left on board the ship was Captain Carlsen, who announced that he would not be leaving until the very end. As a salvage tug was racing to the scene, the fight to save the *Flying Enterprise* could now begin.

The *Greely* was relieved by the destroyer USS *John W. Weeks*, which stood by the listing ship for several days while help was on its way. Every day was a wonder as to how this ship was still afloat as the list seemed to be getting worse, yet she remained afloat. New Year's Day 1952 passed with still no solution to the problem, while Carlsen remained alone on his ship, wondering if he had signed his own death warrant.

At long last, on 3 January 1952, the salvage tug *Turmoil* arrived at the scene and it was quickly established that Carlsen could not manage the salvage operation on that side on his own. The captain of the tug came in close to the *Flying Enterprise* and 27-year-old chief mate Kenneth Dancy leaped on board, grabbing onto the railing and then dashed to attach the towline. Within minutes the ship was secured and the long journey to Falmouth on the southern coast of England began.

The weather was not as bad as it had been so this led to good progress being made, the tug slowly making headway over the coming days, and it actually looked like they just might make it. The list by now was 60 degrees yet still the stricken vessel remained afloat: if they could just make it to a sheltered area or harbour, they could bring the ship upright in the comfort of a safe port.

The fleet of ships now escorting the *Flying Enterprise* made headline news, the image of the listing cargo ship making the front pages, as millions tuned in to watch the drama that was taking place in the middle of the Atlantic. Fingers were crossed that the ship would make it safely, the images of Carlsen and Dancy together on the ship keeping each other company and making sure the towline was okay, the coverage leaving complete strangers rooting for these unlikely heroes.

But in the early hours of 10 January the seas began to pick up again and the towline parted, leaving the ship once again adrift. With only forty-one miles to go until she reached Falmouth, they fought to save her throughout the day, the efforts being in vain though as the tow could not be reattached and the list increased until the ship was almost completely on her side.

By late afternoon Carlsen and Dancy agreed that the ship could not now be saved and finally abandoned ship, being picked up by the *Turmoil*. As the *Flying Enterprise* took on more water and rolled further over, the stern began to settle and the ship went down. As her hull slipped beneath the waves, the ships in the area sounded their sirens in salute to a ship that had refused to give up.

When they finally reached England, they were treated like heroes, the media eager to tell their stories and everybody fighting to be the first to honour these men who had fought until the end. Carlsen was awarded a medal and celebrated in a ticker-tape parade when he returned to New York City the following week.

The wreck of the *Flying Enterprise* was salvaged by an Italian company soon after the sinking, which led to a lot of conspiracy talk over the real cargo of the ship – especially when you consider the captain refusing to leave and the constant military presence the entire time. Taking into account the salvage operation on such a random cargo, it is no wonder people started to ask questions, although nothing was ever proved and even rumours of gold were just that – rumours.

The *Flying Enterprise* was rediscovered in 2001 and was visited by TV crews who filmed her for a documentary. The wreck lies on her port side at a depth of 276 feet; the images brought back showed the rudder and propeller as well as upper structure and machinery.

Kurt Carlsen went back to sea aboard the *Flying Enterprise II* not long after the loss of his ship and continued his career at sea. He would always be famous for those few weeks over Christmas and New Year when he tried in vain to save his ship. He died in 1989, his ashes taken out to sea and scattered over the wreck of his beloved *Flying Enterprise*.

Chapter 29

Princess Victoria, 1953

As passenger travel increased over time and tickets suddenly became more affordable, the need for ferries for shorter trips became more apparent. As more and more people were travelling by car, there needed to be a way for them to take the same journeys but have the opportunity to bring their own mode of transport with them. Enter the roll-on/roll-off ferry.

The RORO ferry was specifically designed for those taking a sea journey to drive on through a large door at the bow and park on the huge car decks that had several lanes. When the ship was ready for sea, the door was closed and the ship would sail to its destination while the occupants enjoyed the ship's facilities on the crossing. When the ship reached its destination, it would back up to a loading ramp and this time the stern doors would open with the vehicles already facing the right direction. This design was very popular for journeys from Britain across the Irish Sea, North Sea and the English Channel, and in some cases as far away as Spain.

One of the first purpose-built RORO ferries was the *Princess Victoria* which was launched in 1947 from William Denny and Brothers shipyard in Dumbarton, Scotland. She was just less than 310 feet long with a gross tonnage of 2,694. Owned by the British Transport Commission, she was operated by the London, Midland and Scottish Railway company for a year until that was taken over by British Railways. Her route was Stranraer in western Scotland to Larne in Northern Ireland, and she could take over 1,500 passengers plus cargo.

The early morning of 31 January 1953 forecast a storm on the horizon, gale-force winds, with a warning to ships that Captain James Ferguson would ignore as he contemplated his journey from Stranraer. In his seventeen years of being a captain on this particular route, he figured he knew the trip like the back of his hand and everything would be fine. After loading up with 128 passengers and 51 crew, the *Princess Victoria* set sail from the pier at 0745 hours and headed out of Loch Ryan and into the Irish Sea for what looked like a rough journey ahead.

Almost as soon as the ship cleared the loch for the twenty-one-mile crossing, she encountered difficulties when, at 0900 hours, waves smashed into the stern doors and allowed water to enter the car deck. As the crew rushed to survey the damage, it was obvious that the doors were buckled beyond repair and every wave was bringing more of the freezing-cold water rushing in.

The problem with a ship such as the *Princess Victoria* is that car decks on any RORO ferry are large wide-open spaces where the cars sit at one of the lowest points of the ship. Even a small amount of water will rush to one side as soon as the ship rolls, which will immediately make the ship unstable. Just one inch of water over a car deck can capsize a ship this size and this fatal flaw in these types of ships is still an issue today (more on that in another chapter – see *Herald of Free Enterprise*).

With the damage done to the doors there were only two options – continue the journey which they would not likely survive, or turn back to Stranraer which meant she had to turn across the seas and suffer the ship rolling over with damaged stern doors. Incredibly, the ship made the turn successfully, but they now had to worry about bringing the ship safely into harbour; however, with such little distance already covered, the captain had every confidence that this could be achieved.

Radio messages were transmitted for assistance from any tugs in the area. The first distress signals were sent as the ship leaned further over with every passing wave. Passengers put on lifejackets and tried to help bail out the water which was now entering the lounge areas. What they didn't know was that an error had been given in her position and what had been transmitted made sure the nearest rescue lifeboat was now going in the wrong direction.

By 1300 that afternoon another radio message alerted any ships in the area to come to their assistance and that they were being forced to abandon ship, but incredibly the wrong coordinates were given once again. The last radio message was received at 1358 hours and then the ferry went silent.

As ships raced to the scene as best they could in such atrocious weather, the lifeboats on the ferry were being lowered and accidentally dropping their occupants into the sea, with other lifeboats freely floating away empty. The *Princess Victoria* lurched further and further over until the ship had completely turned on her side, finally sinking in the stormy seas minutes later.

When the rescue ships finally got to the site of the sinking, five miles from where they thought she was, only forty-four men were left alive, the Donaghadee Lifeboat *Sir Samuel Kelly* rescuing thirty-three of them. None of the survivors were children, women or crewmembers. With the state of the weather, it is a miracle anybody got out of her alive.

The rescue operation saw many people awarded bravery medals for their conduct in helping those in the sea, including the radio operator David Broadfoot who was posthumously awarded the George Cross for staying at his post right till the end. An inquiry into her loss blamed the structural integrity of the stern doors as well as the arrangements for clearing water from the car deck.

The wreck of the *Princess Victoria* today lies in ninety metres of water just five miles off the Copeland Islands, being first dived on in 1992 when a team carried out an expedition based on survey work previously done by the Royal Navy nearly twenty years previously. The first images of the wreck were transmitted on a TV documentary marking the 40th anniversary of the sinking.

Today a number of memorials remember those lost in the sinking of the *Princess Victoria*, one of them at the port where she sailed from on that fateful morning. While she will never be as famous as other ferry disasters in later years, she will always be remembered as the first major RORO disaster that should have served as a warning of what was to come if this design was not looked into and altered.

Like many shipwrecks that were previously forgotten, this one now has several books written about her and where one can go to remember the 133 lives lost in that storm that sank this ferry, as well as several other vessels over the following days. It is just unfortunate that so many more would die in the coming years that the sinking of the *Princess Victoria* would take a back seat and be the shipwreck that everybody forgot.

Chapter 30

Andrea Doria, 1956

Of all the liners that ever put to sea there was a group of Italian vessels that had no intention of competing with the speed of the larger and more famous ships, so instead their owners made them unique with their exquisite interiors of opulent artwork and fine interior design, making these ships nothing short of floating palaces.

The Italian Line based in the port of Genoa knew that these ships had to be different from what the rest of the world could offer and when the *Andrea Doria* was launched on 16 June 1951, she was the pride of Italy, her name deriving from a local admiral from the 1500s. Her two propellers running off steam turbines gave her 29,083-gross-ton hull a good push at a speed of 23 knots through the Atlantic waves where her passages over to the United States would seal her place on the transatlantic and Mediterranean runs. At 701 feet 5 inches long, she had a sleek black hull with a single funnel which gave her the more modern appearance that would soon put the older liners in the shade when it came to style and grace.

After some machinery problems her maiden voyage was delayed by a month, but when she eventually departed Genoa for New York on 14 January 1953, she hit trouble on the journey. While in mid-Atlantic she was battered by a ferocious storm that caused her to take on a heavy list, arriving at her destination at a 28-degree angle much to the horror of those watching. Incredibly, she was only a bit later than the ETA, despite the bad weather and the listing issue, the trip taking just nine days in total.

Over the next few years, she carried thousands of passengers who marvelled at her interior and her style. She became quite a favourite for many passengers and crew alike, and her 1,200-passenger capacity was always fully subscribed.

On 17 July 1956, she sailed from Genoa, and after brief stops at Cannes, Naples and Gibraltar to pick up more passengers, she headed west into the Atlantic like she had done many times before – this was actually her fifty-first westbound voyage to New York, and she had on board 1,134 passengers and 572 crew.

The voyage went without a problem until the night of 25 July when she was off Nantucket and heading into thick fog which continued for several hours. In the meantime, the *Stockholm*, a 525-foot-long Swedish liner of 12,165 gross tons, had just left her berth in New York and was now heading east to Gothenburg, Sweden, with 534 passengers and a crew of 208. Also entering the fog, *Stockholm* carried on steaming at normal speed without slowing down, the *Andrea Doria* only reducing speed very slightly and neither overly concerned of anything untoward.

The two ships were now heading towards each other at almost full speed. At 2245 hours they began seeing each other on their Radar screens, but for some reason both ships misread which direction the other was heading and each chose the opposite path to the other – *Andrea Doria* intended to pass the mystery ship starboard-to-starboard whereas the *Stockholm* planned a port-to-port pass. The two ships were now on a collision course.

At around 2310 hours the two ships appeared to each other in the fog but it was too late, a final attempt to avoid a collision was in vain as the bow of the *Stockholm* tore into the starboard side of the *Andrea Doria* and ripped open the side of the ship like a knife through hot butter.

As the *Stockholm* broke free, her bow had been torn apart and she was in a bad way, but the *Andrea Doria* had been opened up to the sea and immediately took on a list as water flowed freely into her compartments. An evacuation was ordered as injured passengers made their way to the upper deck to the lifeboats which now swung too far outward to be of any use; it was obvious that the ship was in grave danger of sinking with all her complement on board. A distress call was sent out and the rescue operation began.

All ships in the area turned towards the scene of the collision and prepared their own boats for what looked like an immense rescue involving over 1,600 people. The first ship to respond was the damaged *Stockholm*, which prepared for her own survivors to be brought on board once it was determined that she wasn't sinking from the loss of her bow section.

Suddenly the fog lifted and out of the gloom the lights of the French Line's *Île de France* burst onto the scene to a euphoric reaction from those who feared that all was lost, and together with the United States Coast Guard, the passengers were slowly taken off the stricken *Andrea Doria*.

On board the *Stockholm* it was found that a miracle had occurred when crew surveyed the damage to their ship. A young girl named Linda Morgan was found in the wreckage of the bow. She had actually been on board the *Andrea Doria* asleep in her bed when the collision had led to her being scooped out of her bed and trapped on the *Stockholm*. She was alive and only slightly injured.

By around 0900 the following morning, the *Andrea Doria* was a ghost ship, abandoned and listing, surrounded by rescue ships. Her list increased until she was on her side, her bow sliding down first, leaving her port propeller the last thing to be seen, along with her name on the stern. With the ship gone, the survivors were taken to New York by their respective rescue ships.

The sinking of the *Andrea Doria* was eventually blamed on both ships whereby fault was found in several operating procedures carried out that night which led to the deaths of forty-six on board the *Andrea Doria* and a further five on the *Stockholm*.

The wreck is today a popular dive for those who are willing to meet the technical challenge that is the fifty metres of water which mask the currents and dangers lurking beneath the surface. The ship is on her starboard side in one piece and presents an incredible sight, but one that has also been met with tragedy over the years: at the time of writing twenty-two people have died while exploring her; it seems that no matter how safe the dive plan is, the *Andrea Doria* will continue to be dangerous.

Ironically, the *Stockholm* was repaired and put back into service, having several name changes over the years. Today she is still going strong as the *Astoria*, owned by Cruise & Maritime Voyages (CMV) operating out of Portugal, with talks of her retirement taking place in the autumn of 2020, making her the world's oldest cruise ship still in service.

In a final twist to the story, in 2020 a dive team located the bow of the *Stockholm* at the place where the two ships collided. Sixty feet long and at a depth of 250 feet, this crumpled piece of wreckage is the final piece of the puzzle in this dramatic sea story.

Chapter 31

Pamir, 1957

With the birth of the steamship and the opening up of new opportunities for ships to go much faster and much further than ever before, it was only a matter of time before the great sailing ships became obsolete, one by one being replaced by the metal, fuel-burning tramp steamers and liners until very few of them were left in the world.

As the large sailing vessels dwindled, those left had uniqueness and an individuality that was unmatched, such as the *Cutty Sark* (now on display in London) and the *Pamir*. When they were first brought into service, they were the best of the best, but as the years went by, they started to show their age and became expensive to maintain.

The *Pamir* was a four-masted barque of 3,020 gross tons, measuring 375 feet long, with her masts towering 168 feet above her decks; when she was fully rigged with all sails billowing, she was quite a sight to see. Built in 1905 at the Blohm & Voss shipyard in Hamburg, Germany, she began conducting voyages to Chile which would take her around nine or ten weeks one way.

When the First World War broke out, she stayed in port in the Canary Islands until 1920, when she was allowed back to Hamburg and soon handed over to Italy as war reparations, but she was not used and sat around for the next four years off Naples. In 1924, she was purchased by her original owners who put her back on her old jobs which lasted until she was sold again in 1931 to the Erikson Line of Finland, which had her running to and from Australia.

It was during the Second World War that *Pamir* was again seized in a time of conflict, this time by the New Zealand government as a prize of war, to use the ship on other voyages around the world to several ports in the USA and Canada. She was returned to the Erikson Line in 1948 who sold her upon the death of the owner in 1951 and she was towed to Antwerp for scrapping.

But in the nick of time she was purchased by a man named Heinz Schliewen who had sailed on her in the 1920s and saved the ship from being dismantled. Instead, she was fitted out with all-new modern technology, including an auxiliary engine, communications systems, a refrigeration unit and water-ballast tanks.

Although she still carried cargo, her main role now was a sailing training vessel which kept the history of the ship alive. Unfortunately, money was tight and the ship was allowed to deteriorate over time with regular leaks and a continuous problem with corrosion, the lack of profits not being able to keep up with the maintenance required for such an old ship.

On 10 August 1957, the *Pamir* sailed from Buenos Aires, Argentina, bound for Hamburg with a cargo of barley and eighty-six people on board, fifty-two of them being cadets. By 21 September she had reached the middle of the Atlantic when she was caught in bad weather, in this case Hurricane Carrie. The strength of the storm seems to have left her with a significant list to port which, together with her questionable structural integrity, would have left her open to the elements and most likely to have let water into the ship.

There were several issues with the voyage that were known to have caused concern. The radio operator had more than one role on board, so this meant that instead of receiving storm warnings, he was busy doing other things ... who knows how many important ones were missed in this time. When passing ships called her on the radio, they got no response, almost as if she was a ghost ship.

As *Pamir* listed further, the lifeboats proved useless as they were thrust underwater while those on the other side were on top of the hull. A distress signal was picked up by a British coastal station, stunning the operator when it was revealed that she was listing too far over to be righted. Nothing more was heard soon after that.

As the masts broke away and everything below decks shifted further over, the cadets and crew desperately clung to the side of the ship, the wreckage and anything else that might save their lives, but they knew it was now hopeless. *Pamir* rolled fully over and stayed upside down, adrift for a short while, before finally disappearing beneath the stormy Atlantic around 600 miles from the Azores.

The search for survivors lasted nine days and all that was located were two lifeboats with four crew and two cadets aboard; more wreckage and empty boats were found nearby but no sign of life of the other eighty people was ever found.

The cause of the sinking seemed almost open and shut. The state of the ship as well as reports that the cargo of grain was not properly secured, therefore easily moved as the ship rolled over, which led to her listing without being able to recover. With grain in the empty ballast tanks, had these been flooded, it would have lowered the centre of gravity and perhaps have righted the list and possibly saved the ship, but this was not done.

Today there are very few ships that can be put into the same class as *Pamir*: she really was one of the last of her kind and it was fair play to the owner who saved her from the scrapheap to try and save the nostalgia of the vessel and breathe new life into her. Unfortunately, running a ship like this just took up any spare time and money, her loss becoming a German national tragedy and making front-page headlines around the world.

A number of plaques today commemorate the eighty dead of the *Pamir*, including Wellington (New Zealand) and the German cities of Lubeck and Hamburg. As the name of this fine vessel fades from history as one of the last major sailing vessel disasters, it is important to keep her story alive and hope that one day, someone will give her the attention she so deserves and head out to look for the wreck. Until that day comes, we can only imagine what she looks like on the seabed, several miles down.

Chapter 32

Torrey Canyon, 1967

With any shipwreck the main problem is first evacuating the people on board and then saving the ship, if possible. If the ship sinks, then most of the time it is a simple case of sorting out the insurance and then it is forgotten about. But what if a ship sank and the main issue wasn't this ... what if the cargo presents a catastrophe worse than the shipwreck itself? For this we introduce one such wreck, the *Torrey Canyon*.

At 974.4 feet long and over 61,000 gross tons, this ship was a massive oil tanker with a capacity for 120,000 tons of crude oil. She was one of many of these large ships that seemed to be increasing in numbers as the rise in oil production necessitated a larger field of transportation. Built in Newport News, USA, in 1959, she was operated by British Petroleum and had already gone through a process in Japan in 1965 to double her carrying capacity.

She set sail from Mina in the Persian Gulf state of Kuwait on 19 February 1967, with her tanks full of crude oil, bound for the Milford Haven terminal in Wales. A month later, the *Torrey Canyon* was not far from her final destination approaching the southwest coast of England. It was around 0850 hours on the morning of 18 March, just off the Isles of Scilly, when the captain decided it would be a good idea to alter course, away from the shipping channel and take a short cut, which would bring the ship closer to shore but would save him some time in the long run. The tanker had been left on auto pilot; the helmsman was unaware of this, more of a design fault than the person at the wheel who would not know which selection had been made unless he was told about it or physically did it himself.

With a shuddering jolt the huge bulk of the *Torrey Canyon* grounded on the rocks at the Seven Stones Reef and came to a stop. The ship was now in dire straits, her hull was damaged and large amounts of oil began seeping into the sea. The ship had to be rescued as soon as possible or the consequences were unthinkable.

A black slick started spreading around the tanker and heading out to sea, not a good situation. That evening attempts to move the ship failed and so the crew were rescued by lifeboats. Within twenty-four hours only her captain, Pastrengo Rugiati, remained on board with three of his crew. Helicopters were starting to monitor the spread of the oil, which by now was twenty miles long and the ship was no further on from being pulled off the rocks.

Across the south coast came a call for assistance, including detergent, as it was feared that the oil would start coming onto the beaches before too long. A salvage crew was mobilized to try and save the ship while she was still in one piece.

By 21 March the slick had spread 100 miles and the race to save the ship was now bordering on desperation, as with every hour that passed more and more crude oil leaked into the sea. A fleet of small vessels were ferrying chemicals out to fight the slicks, and the Royal Navy had warships such as the destroyer HMS *Barrosa* in the area to monitor the operation and assist in dealing with the oil. But it seemed to be a lost cause. That night the captain was taken off, much to his sadness at having failed to save his ship, and brought with his crew to the salvage tug *Titan* which was closing the gap between them and the wreck.

The tugs owners, a Dutch salvage team, were now on site and immediately got to work boarding the ship. The eighteen-man crew was led by 38-year-old Captain Albert Stal; their first task was to inspect the vessel to see what could be done to drag her from the rocks. They started pumping compressed air into her engine room to try and force the water out and get the ship off the rocks. But suddenly a large explosion rocked the vessel, injuring eleven crew and blowing several of them overboard. They were picked up by the *Titan* but sadly Captain Stal, struck by flying wreckage, died on board the tug soon after.

All was not lost though, as 22 March brought news that the battle to break up the oil slicks was being won, slowly but surely. But at the same time the first sighting of affected wildlife was a flock of gulls covered in black oil. The race was still very much on to stop the oil from reaching the shore.

Two days later the tanker was still unmoved from the rocks as the oil finally reached the beaches of Cornwall, after six days of struggling to contain the slick and attempting to free the tanker. But on Sunday, 26 March, it was all over: the *Torrey Canyon* broke her back and released the vast bulk of her cargo into the sea in one foul tide. Although some tanks still held out, it wouldn't be for long before they too collapsed.

This was now a monumental disaster. With every wave that hit the south coast beaches, a new tide of black sludge mixed with dead wildlife washed in with it. The task to clean this up was overwhelming as the wreck of the *Torrey Canyon* broke up and her sad remains were on the front pages of the newspapers.

The government had to make a decision that would be both unpopular and necessary – to bomb the oil slicks out at sea and burn them up before the rest of it caused further damage. At dawn on 28 March, eight Royal Navy Buccaneer jets took off and headed to the site, dropping bombs on the vast slicks where the resulting explosions set off a conflagration with thick black smoke and flames leaping hundreds of feet into the air.

This was followed by Hawker Hunters dropping kerosene which burned furiously, a mission objective that thankfully has not had to be used since. This went on for two days but by then the damage to the beaches was irreversible.

The clean-up operation extended as far as the Channel Islands, with Guernsey utilizing a disused quarry to contain the oil that was siphoned into to be dealt with later. This still had oil in by 2010 when the final cleaning was being undertaken, forty-three years after the disaster.

Today the wreck of the *Torrey Canyon* is only thirty metres down, broken up where she lay following the grounding and subsequent bombing raids. She remains the largest oil spill in the UK and was (at the time) the biggest ever shipwreck. She remains today the largest wreck off the British coast.

The lessons of the disaster were learned fast, for the next few decades would see a sharp influx of oil tanker groundings, with each having its own unique problems. But the fundamentals were the same – the inability to stop the flow of oil from a massive ship with a hole in the side.

Chapter 33

Seawise University, 1972

Most people will be unfamiliar with the ship that ended her life as the *Seawise University*, because by then she had already had a stellar career under a previous name. Most people today still refer to her by her previous existence as an ocean liner rather than a floating place of study; therefore, she will still be known as the RMS *Queen Elizabeth* of the Cunard Line.

With the older liners like the *Aquitania*, *Mauritania* and the *Berengaria* showing their age, the Cunard Line needed some new ships that would bring the company back up to speed with the world's transatlantic liner industry, and therefore two new ships were designed for that reason. The *Queen Mary* and the *Queen Elizabeth* were longer than any they had previously ordered but the fallout from the worldwide depression meant that building these was slow going.

The *Queen Mary* was eventually finished and sailed on her maiden voyage in 1936. The *Queen Elizabeth* however, was not ready until the Second World War had already broken out. She had been launched in 1938 but was still in the builder's yard being fitted out when the government requisitioned her for military use as a troop transport.

Quickly finishing the jobs on her to make her seaworthy, she sailed, painted in battleship grey, on 3 March 1940 for a secret mission to New York, avoiding all contact with anything and anybody on the way. When she arrived six days later, she was berthed next to both the *Queen Mary* and the *Normandie*, quite a sight for anybody passing by!

From that moment on her role was to carry personnel to all the different war zones around the world, which took her to Singapore, South Africa, the Caribbean, Canada and Australia. By the time America entered the war, the two Cunard liners were back on the transatlantic route taking US military to the United Kingdom. By the time the war was over she had carried over three quarters of a million personnel safely to their destinations.

She was now ready to be fitted out for her intended role – a luxury liner. While her running partner was repatriating troops and GI brides back to the USA, the *Queen Elizabeth* was being converted back to how she was meant to be. Only now was she able to do actual trials and plan for a maiden voyage. The real Queen Elizabeth and her two daughters, Princesses Margaret and Elizabeth (the future Queen), were on board at one stage, taking the ship's wheel and seeing how a ship of such magnitude was tested and helping record the results.

The liner passed all the tests and eventually sailed on her maiden passenger voyage on 16 October 1946, and for the next twenty years she delighted all those who sailed in her. At over 83,000 gross tons and 1,031 feet long, she was the biggest liner in the world at the time of her building, eclipsing the *Queen Mary* by a mere twelve feet.

With her sleek black hull and two funnels painted in Cunard red with a black top, her image was everywhere and she became one of the most beloved liners in the world. But by the early 1960s the problem facing both liners was the progress of technology. When the jet airliner was introduced for commercial travel soon after the war ended, it was greeted with excitement, although many people had a fear of flying. After several teething problems, jetliners started offering a quick and simple way to get from point A to point B without having to spend days on end aboard a ship rocking backwards and forwards. The popularity of the airliner industry grew apace with the carrying capacity of the aircraft involved, and it soon became apparent that the passenger liner industry would suffer as a result.

Cunard fitted out the two ships as cruise liners, still covering the same routes, but this time the liner itself was the holiday. This was successful but not enough to entice the same number of customers pre-jetliner days.

The two ships were now over thirty years old and needed replacing. The new *Queen Elizabeth 2* – affectionately nicknamed *QE2* – was ordered specifically for the cruise industry and the two older liners were put up for sale. The *Queen Mary* was sold and went over to Long Beach, California, where she would later open up as a hotel, which is still operating today.

The *Queen Elizabeth* was sold on auction in 1970 to Hong Kong businessman C.Y. Tung who already owned several large vessels. His idea was to have the ship anchored in Hong Kong harbour and fitted out as a floating university. Her hull was painted white and she was renamed

Seawise University, with high hopes that the ship would have a new lease of life and an exciting future.

But this was not meant to be, as during the conversion process, on 9 January 1972, the *Seawise University* caught fire. Nobody really knows what happened: some suggest it was arson as part of an insurance fraud, others say it was started by C.Y. Tung's business rival, but nothing has ever been proved.

As local fire boats sprayed the ship, the water displacement within the compartments caused the ship to become unstable and the blazing wreck slowly leaned over onto her starboard side, until all that was left was a charred, burned-out hulk resting half-sunk in the harbour. The fire made front-page news around the world.

The wreck was featured in the James Bond film, *The Man with the Golden Gun*, where MI6 had a secret base within the wreck that also housed Q's technology lab. But over the years she was slowly broken up for scrap until all that was left was what lay beneath the surface, some say nearly half the wreck.

Land reclamation eventually saw her buried under what is now Container Terminal 9, a beautiful and popular ship now lying under the concrete of a working port. Who knows if we will see her again in our lifetime, but for her service during both wartime and peace, the *Queen Elizabeth* will always be remembered.

Chapter 34

Edmund Fitzgerald, 1975

In 1976, a Canadian folk singer released a single that paid tribute to the events of the previous November, hitting the number one spot in the Canadian charts and number two in the United States, telling the story of a ship and her crew caught in a storm.

In a musty old hall in Detroit they prayed,
In the maritime sailors' cathedral
The church bell chimed 'til it rang twenty-nine times
For each man on the Edmund Fitzgerald

went the final verse of the Gordon Lightfoot song. Because of this music, many more people know the name of the *Edmund Fitzgerald* than any other shipwreck in the Great Lakes, but her story is not fiction – it is one of true-life tragedy and mystery.

Launched in 1958, the freighter was designed especially for working the five Great Lakes that are situated at the very top of the United States and the bottom of Canada, a divide that has led to hundreds of trade routes being established over the years and, as with every such route, has become home to thousands of shipwrecks.

At 729 feet long, she was over 13,000 gross tons and carried cargoes of ore. Her odd shape – a regular tanker but with a forward bridge as well as her length – made her the largest ship operating on the Lakes at the time. Whenever a ship breaks the record for the title of largest ship here, it get the unofficial title of 'Queen of the Great Lakes', something the *Edmund Fitzgerald* held for only a year before a new ship claimed the record by a size difference of just a few inches.

Over the next seventeen years the *Edmund Fitzgerald* did some 748 round trips, totalling the equivalent of forty-four trips round the world, setting new records for the tonnage of iron ore she could carry. She was a successful vessel and earned a number of affectionate nicknames such as

'Mighty Fitz' and 'Big Fitz', amongst others. Apart from a few mishaps later in her career – including collision and running aground several times – she was a favourite of those watching vessels sail by.

On the afternoon of 9 November 1975, she sailed from Superior, Wisconsin, with a cargo of taconite ore pellets. There was talk of a storm, but she was expected to pass that clear by the following day. But that night the storm had altered course somewhat and warnings put the storm across the whole of Lake Superior, right into the path of several vessels, including *Edmund Fitzgerald*.

With twenty-nine people on board, she encountered the storm as expected early on the morning of 10 November. She was sighted by another vessel, the *Arthur M. Anderson*, later that day. Radio reports to this same vessel suggested that the ship had suffered slight damage and that she was taking on water, but no distress signal was sent to give any indication that the ship couldn't handle what was being thrown at her. Both the *Anderson* and the *Fitzgerald* had similar cargoes and had departed from the same port just hours apart.

By now the *Anderson* was struggling with the waves as they smashed into her side, tossing the vessel about. The winds reached around 67mph that afternoon with the *Anderson* contacting the *Fitzgerald* to ask if they were alright. 'We're holding our own,' was the reply. Nothing was ever heard from the *Edmund Fitzgerald* again. By the time the *Anderson* realized that the vessel was no longer on their RADAR, the *Edmund Fitzgerald* had disappeared without trace.

Concerned about the sudden lack of communication, the coastguard was informed that the ship had simply vanished from RADAR and a search was launched in conjunction with the crew of the *Anderson* to comb the area for any signs of the missing ship.

Before long debris was found floating on the surface along with two lifeboats from the *Edmund Fitzgerald*, confirmation that the ship was lost. A further search revealed nothing else, no sign of a ship of that size and no sign of the twenty-nine crew.

When the storm passed, a coastguard vessel conducted a search using SONAR and, less than two weeks after the ship went down, it located two large objects on the seabed in the area where she had last been seen. With all indications suggesting that this was the *Edmund Fitzgerald*, a further expedition was launched the following May when cameras were sent down to confirm her identity, something which didn't take long when the name was spelled out plain to see on the stern. The destruction of this vessel and the suddenness of her loss shocked Canada.

Her wreck was located in two halves, the stern upside down, but the bow upright as if still sailing through the mud that now trapped her, over 500 feet beneath the waves. An investigation suggested that the cause of the sinking was the ineffective hatch closing which led to flooding during the storm.

The truth of what happened to this record-breaking ship may never be known, but more expeditions to the seabed to investigate the wreck have led to some significant footage of her remains and several items salvaged for the local museums. Her bell is today on display at the Great Lakes Shipwreck Museum.

So, with the tragedy of the sinking, the mystery of its cause and mourning the loss of her crew, it seems valid to point out how a folk singer wrote up her story in song and made the name of this cargo ship a household name. With no bodies ever recovered, the song reflects on this in the final lines:

> *'Superior,' they said, 'never gives up her dead*
> *When the gales of November come early.'*

Chapter 35

Derbyshire, 1980

Of all the vessels sailing today, the bulk carrier is one of the most underrated workhorses of the world. With thousands of these massive ships steadily taking vast amounts of cargo from port to port, it is only inevitable that now and again one of them will meet danger and be lost. But for the 91,655-gross-ton *Derbyshire*, this was one of several of a certain type to sink and cause major concern.

Built in 1975 as the *Liverpool Bridge*, she was 965 feet 3 inches long; she was designed to carry cargoes of iron ore, dry bulk items much like how oil tankers carry their cargo, even down to both looking similar from a distance. She was built by Swan Hunter in Tyne and Wear but owned by the Bibby Line of Liverpool, a company that had grown from strength to strength over the decades, with the new-style ships delivering mass freight to ports across all corners of the earth.

The *Liverpool Bridge* was not a fast ship: her size meant that a speed of only around 15 knots could be achieved but this was good considering how long it takes for such vessels to come to a stop in an emergency.

In 1978 the ship was renamed the *Derbyshire* and continued to ply her trade on long-haul voyages across the globe.

On 11 July 1980, she departed from Sept-Îles in Canada bound for Kawasaki in Japan with a cargo of 157,446 tons of iron ore in her holds. Making sure she got there safely was her forty-two-strong crew, along with two of the crew's wives who were also making the trip. As the vessel slowly made its way across the Pacific, a storm was brewing that was growing in strength, eventually being given the name Typhoon Orchid when the winds increased significantly. As the *Derbyshire* transited the South China Sea, she would have been feeling the effects of the bad weather but it was nothing new for a ship of such size and there was no reason why the crew should be concerned.

But by 10 September nothing was ever heard from the *Derbyshire* again. When she failed to arrive at her destination five days later, a huge search and rescue operation was launched at the ship's last known position. Apart from some oil on the surface, the massive vessel seemed to have simply vanished without trace. Weeks later a lifeboat was located by a passing ship confirming that the vessel had met with disaster, but by then it was common knowledge.

Many theories arose over the years as to what could have happened to her, the first and most obvious being that she was battered by Typhoon Orchid and eventually overwhelmed by the heavy seas and sank. But other explanations caused more concern and these came from not the *Derbyshire*, but her sister ships of the same class. The first one was the *Tyne Bridge,* when eighteen months after the sinking of her sister, she was making her way across the North Sea. Suddenly a crack appeared in the deck forward of the superstructure at Frame number 65. When examined it was found that several cracks had appeared, leading to major structural faults.

This didn't seem to be a one-off either. In 1986, the *Kowloon Bridge* was making her way from Canada to Scotland when she developed the same kind of crack in her hull. After further complications she ended up running aground off West Cork, Ireland, where she broke into three and sank, one of the breaks being at Frame 65. The wreck of the *Kowloon Bridge* led to concerns that the *Derbyshire* had also developed major structural damage and had been lost as a result.

The only thing that would settle the argument was if the wreck was located, but with no last reported position, where could you even start looking? Despite the ship being massive, it was still like searching for a needle in a haystack. Thankfully, wreck hunter David Mearns offered his services after pleas and funding from the International Transport Workers' Federation, along with the Derbyshire Family Association, an organization set up to find out the truth about what had happened to their loved ones. They needed answers and they needed them now: they had already waited fourteen years and had got nowhere.

In June 1994, Mearns and his team set off on what seemed an impossible task and locate the wreck of the *Derbyshire* in just eight days, the maximum amount of time that could be afforded. Incredibly, on the last leg of the expedition, a target was located two and a half miles down on the seabed, south of Japan. Mearns immediately deployed the Remotely Operated Vehicle (ROV) *Magellan* to hopefully positively identify their target.

What seemed impossible turned into a dramatic twist when the letters SHIRE spelled out on the broken stern confirmed the identity of the wreck, but the state of the ship left nobody in doubt that while one mystery was solved, another was uncovered.

The wreck of the *Derbyshire* was a complete mess, with seven large sections and thousands of pieces scattered across the seabed, more like a scrapyard than a shipwreck. A new expedition was launched which conducted a more detailed survey and took tens of thousands of photographs, enough evidence to reopen the inquiry which had, in 1987, blamed the crew for bad seamanship.

As the new inquiry was launched in 2000, evidence was submitted that showed the ship had been flooding due to an inadequate hatch cover near the bow, allowing water in and slowly filling the ship up with water until she was down by the bow. The resulting floods destroyed other hatches along the ship until she went down and imploded with the amount of pressure put on her bulkheads.

With the crew cleared of blame, the families could now rest easy and grieve for their loved ones without having to fight for justice. Today a memorial stands in a Liverpool churchyard to commemorate the forty-four who died on board the *Derbyshire*, a place that is covered in flowers every anniversary and will be so for many years to come.

What is still concerning is the number of bulk carriers that continued to go down long after the loss of the *Derbyshire* and the *Kowloon Bridge*. Figures put the toll at 300 of these huge ships with the loss of over 1,000 crew. As a class of ship goes, especially given the size of the vessels, this is a figure that is far too high to ignore.

Chapter 36

General Belgrano, 1982

Like Midway and Pearl Harbor, a campaign or event that includes several ships meeting their doom is a tricky one when it comes to writing about just one. When word came through that the Argentine junta had invaded the UK-owned Falkland Islands and South Georgia in the South Atlantic in April 1982, the resulting campaign saw hundreds of people killed and a fair few good ships sunk on both sides in the fighting.

The events surrounding the loss of the ARA *General Belgrano* have been talked and written about for almost four decades and any researcher could easily disappear down a rabbit warren when searching for the truth as to what happened. But this is the story of the Falklands campaign and the loss of the *General Belgrano* in a brief chapter.

Launched in Camden, New Jersey, in March 1938, she was originally called the USS *Phoenix*, a Brooklyn-class light cruiser armed with fifteen 6-inch guns on five turrets (three forward, two aft). At 608.3 feet long, she displaced 9,575 tons and had a complement of around 1,138 crew.

On 7 December 1941, she was anchored in Pearl Harbor when the Japanese attacked. As ships started blowing up and sinking, the *Phoenix* opened fire on the enemy aircraft and quickly got underway; a famous photograph of her was released showing her completely undamaged with chaos and ships sinking all around her. That afternoon she left Pearl and went on the hunt for the Japanese fleet.

For the next few years, she took part in the Pacific campaign, including the Philippines and escort duties. She survived the war and was placed in reserve in February 1946.

For the next five years she was laid up until Argentina purchased her in 1951 and the *Phoenix* was renamed *Diecisiete de Octubre* (17th of October).

With the government of Argentina unstable, she took part in the 1955 coup which overthrew President Juan Perón (ironically, she was named after an important date in his party's calendar), and renamed ARA *General Belgrano*, after the country's founding father, Manuel Belgrano. She was fitted out with the Sea Cat missile system in 1968.

When Argentina seized the Falklands on 2 April 1982, British Prime Minister Margaret Thatcher sent the Royal Navy to take the islands back. A large fleet sailed, consisting of two aircraft carriers, several destroyers, frigates, submarines, supply ships, landing platform docks and even ferries and liners to be used as troop transports and hospital ships (*Canberra*, *QE2* and *Uganda* to name a few).

The British declared the area around the Falklands a Maritime Exclusion Zone of 200 nautical miles, which meant that any enemy vessel in the area would be sunk. One of the submarines patrolling this zone was HMS *Conqueror*, a Churchill-class nuclear-powered submarine that had arrived unseen and was ready to strike without warning.

The zone was then upgraded to a Total Exclusion Zone, which meant that any ship in the area, even if it was not Argentinean, could be sunk. Very close to the outer limits of this zone was an Argentine task force comprised of two destroyers and the *General Belgrano*, under orders to attack the British fleet the following day. This signal was intercepted by the British which now put the Argentinean ships at the top of the priority list for targeting.

The *Conqueror* had been shadowing the task force since 30 April and a message was sent to the highest level of government to report on their activities. As they were outside the official TEZ, they sought permission to attack. The approval came from Thatcher herself. The submarine got herself into position and, at 1557 hours on 2 May 1982, she fired three conventional torpedoes at the *General Belgrano*. The first torpedo struck the ship's bow which blew it completely off; incredibly, the forward bulkheads held strong, but the second torpedo struck further aft and exploded internally, causing huge fires and ripping into several decks above.

The old cruiser was now sinking and, as soon as the damage was appreciated, just twenty minutes after the explosions, Captain Hector Bonzo ordered abandon ship. Life rafts were deployed and the crew raced to evacuate but without panic. Incredibly, the escorting vessels were unaware of what had happened, even though it is now thought that the *Conqueror's* third torpedo actually hit one of them but failed to explode.

By the time it was realized that the *General Belgrano* had actually gone down, it was already getting dark with worsening weather, the survivors being tossed about in orange rafts drifting further and further apart. Eventually ships raced to the scene and found a total of 772 people alive, leaving 323 dead, including two civilians.

The next few months would see many other ships sunk, including destroyers HMS *Sheffield* two days later, HMS *Coventry* on 25 May, frigate HMS *Ardent* on 21 May, HMS *Antelope* on 22 May, cargo vessel *Atlantic Conveyor* on 25 May and the landing ship *RFA Sir Galahad* with the landing craft *F4* on 8 June.

Argentina lost seven other minor vessels as well as the submarine *Santa Fe*. While each side would feel the loss of several ships, the sinking of the *General Belgrano* would be the worst. The controversy over her sinking led many to believe that Britain had committed a war crime; however, this was later confirmed by many Argentines that the ship was planning to launch an attack and that the sinking was a legitimate act of war, endorsed by Captain Bonzo himself.

The results of this sinking meant that Argentina could no longer risk her navy in an area where submarines of this calibre were lurking. Their aircraft carrier and all the escort ships turned about and headed back to port. Their navy would now be completely absent from the conflict. On 14 June 1982, the Argentine military surrendered but not before the deaths of 649 Argentineans, 255 British and 3 Falkland Islanders. One of Britain's tabloid newspapers (*The Sun*) first reported the sinking of *General Belgrano* with the headline 'Gotcha' with misguided reports as to the details, but this became one of the most famous front-page headlines in history.

In 2003, an expedition sponsored by National Geographic put to sea to attempt to locate the wreck and bring back the first images of the ship on the seabed; on board were veterans from both *General Belgrano* and HMS *Conqueror*. At first, video footage showed the Argentinians retaining some bitterness over the conflict, but by the end of the expedition they all parted ways, firm friends, as are now many others who fought against each other in 1982. After several weeks of bad weather, the expedition failed to find the lost cruiser, and so she remains undiscovered to this day.

Chapter 37

Herald of Free Enterprise, 1987

Thirty-four years had passed since the sinking of the RORO car ferry *Princess Victoria* and nothing had changed in terms of the problem that arose from water on a car deck making a ship of such design so unstable that it would sink in minutes. Dozens of ferries like this around the world had met their end with the free surface effect of flooding no matter how the water would enter.

Townsend Thoresen was the owner of such ferries: the shipping company had been launching a steadily increasing fleet for years with services from all the major UK ports to Belgium, France and Holland. Their distinctive red ferries and unique design became very familiar on the shipping lanes and easily recognizable, but one ferry met with disaster in 1982 when the *European Gateway* was involved in a collision with the *Speedlink Vanguard* off Felixstowe and sank. Water had got onto her car deck and, sure enough, the free surface effect turned the ferry completely on her side, killing six people. The image of the ferry on the front pages of the newspapers with the company name emblazoned across the side of the upturned ship was a disaster in every way, but one that was not to be their worst.

In 1980 the company had three new ships delivered, the *Herald of Free Enterprise*, the *Spirit of Free Enterprise* and the *Pride of Free Enterprise* and these vessels quickly became the pride of the Townsend Thoresen fleet. At 432 feet and 9 inches long and 7,951 gross tons, they could carry 1,400 people and up to 350 cars and large long-haul vehicles.

On the evening of Friday, 6 March 1987, the *Herald of Free Enterprise* loaded her vehicles and passengers at the Belgian port of Zeebrugge and prepared for the overnight crossing to Dover on the coast of Kent. Due to the loading ramp on the shore terminal not being designed for that class of ship, the forward ballast tanks had to be filled in order to lower the bow of the ship to accommodate this minor issue. The vehicles loaded without a problem and the ship was ready to go by 1800 hours.

Five minutes later the ship slowly backed away from the terminal and made the turn around. She had on board 459 passengers, 80 crew, 81 cars, 47 lorries and 3 buses. The passengers watched from the windows in the cafeteria and restaurant as the vessel made her way out of the breakwater and into the North Sea.

What nobody on board had realized was that the man who was supposed to close the bow doors was asleep in a cabin, while another crew member who should have checked on him was confident that he had done his job and thought no more about it. The *Herald* began to pick up speed and with the bow still weighted down, water started to wash onto the exposed car deck.

At around 1828 hours, the ferry lurched to one side and everybody on board could tell something was not right, not just a minute and half after leaving the harbour behind. She righted herself and then just as quickly lurched back to port, only this time she did not recover. Everything that could move was thrown from one side of the ship to the other. Plates, food, cutlery, bottles, people, cars … everything went over and several passengers were injured by flying items.

The *Herald of Free Enterprise* fell onto her side and came to a stop on a sandbank. Had she been in deeper water there would have been no hope for her occupants – that sandbank stopped hundreds of people being trapped underwater and drowning.

Nearby, the dredger *Sanderas* noticed the ferry didn't look right: within just forty-five seconds the lights went out and the ship disappeared. The *Sanderas* crew reported what they had seen to the port authority and an alert was sounded that a major disaster was now taking place just half a mile outside the harbour entrance. Every available vessel rushed to the scene and ambulances sped to the harbour to await the injured. This was something that Zeebrugge had never had to deal with.

Deep inside the darkness of the capsized *Herald of Free Enterprise*, survivors were clinging on to anything that would hold them above the water. Lifejackets released ended up forming a barrier on the water that actually was a hindrance rather than helping save lives. The sound of helicopters and rescue workers soon filled the air, but they couldn't come fast enough as the freezing-cold North Sea was quickly having its effect on those trapped within.

One by one the passengers and crew were pulled out and taken on board the rescue vessels, some on the helicopters airlifted straight to shore. The crews worked into the night and by the following day they had successfully rescued over 300 people, but that left a horrifying ending: 193 people had died in the disaster. Daylight showed in plain sight the open bow door exposed for all to see. The cause of the accident was right there; the investigators now had to figure out how this was possible.

The Townsend Thoresen logo and name would now only be famous for this disaster, so her owners redacted the name from all the ferries, and each was repainted and rebranded as P&O.

When all the evidence on the sinking was gathered, a public inquiry blamed the two people responsible down below for making sure the bow doors were closed, and also the captain David Lewry for allowing the ship to proceed to sea without knowing the status of his ship. An inquest later returned a verdict of unlawful killing with the owners, P&O European Ferries, being charged with corporate manslaughter. The case collapsed and caused uproar amongst the families of the victims.

The survivors were in the papers more than expected when it was later found that several of them had been nominated for bravery awards – including one who used himself as a human bridge to allow others to cross a gap to safety.

The wreck of the *Herald of Free Enterprise* was salvaged by Smit Tak and towed into port where she was later sold to Naviera SA Kingstown. Renamed *Flushing Range*, she met a storm off the coast of South Africa and was almost lost, eventually arriving in Taiwan on 22 March 1988 to be dismantled.

Today there are memorials to the sinking of the *Herald of Free Enterprise* in the form of stained-glass windows in two Dover churches, a garden on Marine Parade in Dover and a local church in Zeebrugge. At one of the churches is a list of all her victims as well as her bell on display.

As with any disaster of this scale, her victims will never be forgotten, especially when the image of that bright red ferry lying on her side is imprinted into the minds of anybody who remembers the 1980s.

Chapter 38

Doña Paz, 1987

The Philippines have always been a nation of people who travel by sea, their myriad islands and coasts often requiring the use of one of the many ferry companies that ply their trade carrying thousands of passengers on ships of questionable safety.

In 1980 the *Don Juan* was involved in a collision with an oil tanker and sank. An investigation showed that she was overloaded and 176 people were killed. She was only licensed to carry 864 people: there were 888 survivors alone. But it seemed that history is always destined to repeat itself when lessons are not learned.

The *Himeyuri Maru* was a Japanese ferry launched in 1963, only 305 feet long and 2,324 gross tons. She sailed under the Japanese flag for twelve years before being sold to Sulpicio Lines of Manila and renamed the *Don Sulpicio*; in 1981 she was renamed the *Doña Paz*. She already had a colourful history, salvaged after a 1979 fire where she was beached and declared a constructive total loss. The owners salvaged her and put her back to sea under her new name.

The *Doña Paz* was licensed to carry just over 1,500 passengers with a crew of 66. Her twice-weekly journeys from Manila to Tacloban and Catbalogan would satisfy her passengers as a means to an end: these were far from luxury ferries and often overcrowded.

In the early morning of 20 December 1987, the ship departed Tacloban for Manila via Catbalogan in a fairly rough sea but nothing to worry about. As the ship sailed into the late evening, an oil tanker named *Vector* was nearby carrying a cargo of highly flammable products, including gasoline, from Bataan to Masbate. The *Vector* was a 170-foot-long ship of only 629 gross tons, being crewed by only thirteen people. The two ships would normally pass each other without an issue, but tonight the crew of the *Doña Paz* were having a party with loud music on the ship's bridge, the captain being one of those attending. Other crewmembers were watching television or drinking beer.

At around 2230 that night, the ships were in the Tablas Strait and regardless of what was going on inside both ships, the two of them collided with devastating effect. The crash ignited the cargo of the *Vector* and huge explosions rocked the tanker, quickly spreading onto the *Doña Paz* and causing massive conflagrations on both vessels.

The vessels parted and the crews of the two flaming ships wasted no time in abandoning them. Panic ensued with the flames spreading very quickly. The storage lockers for the lifejackets were locked and people started jumping overboard to avoid a fiery death. At least with the blackness of the sea, they stood a chance, albeit a slight one, of survival.

A nearby ship, the *Don Claudio*, saw the explosions in the distance and immediately raced to help, getting as close as possible within an hour and began pulling survivors out of the water, but just twenty-seven people were picked up alive: two from the *Vector* and the rest from the *Doña Paz*. The ferry went down after just two hours, the *Vector* following suit two hours later.

What followed was chaos as the Philippine authorities were not informed of the disaster for eight hours. A further eight hours elapsed before a search and rescue operation was launched. By this time everybody who had not already been picked up was dead. The death toll was shocking: it was revealed that 1,583 passengers and 58 crew had been on board at the time of the collision, with only 25 survivors (one wasn't accounted for until 2012 when she was revealed so officially there were only 24 from *Doña Paz* at this time).

But this was where confusion started. Of the twenty-four passengers who had survived, only five had been on the passenger manifest. Of twenty-one bodies recovered, only one was on the manifest. Relatives of missing passengers started turning up at the offices of the Sulpicio Lines and demanding answers. Hundreds of people claimed that their relatives had booked passage for the Christmas holidays on the *Doña Paz* had not returned Already the sinking had made worldwide headlines, but the revelation to come would make it all the more shocking.

It took over a week on from the disaster before the ferry company admitted that there were many people on board the ship who had not been on the manifest. Young children were not on the list, illegal ticket holders and other complimentary tickets too. The result was a staggering toll of 4,374 dead, as well as the 11 crew on the *Vector*. This made the sinking of the *Doña Paz* the world's worst peacetime maritime disaster ever, a Christmas that the Philippines would never forget.

As the investigation continued it was found out that the negligence of the crew and their lax approach to safety were a major factor in the collision and the overcrowding was confirmed by the few survivors who saw the huge number of people sleeping in corridors and several to a bed with some even on the upper deck. Not only that, the tanker *Vector* had problems with her rudder and several members of crew were underqualified, with the vessel's licence already having expired. In this tragedy of epic proportions, both ships were to blame for such a massive loss of life in this national disaster – although a court ruled that it was the tanker at fault for the collision itself. Again, history was never learned and ferries in the Philippines continue to sink year after year, often with ridiculously high death tolls.

In April 2019, underwater search teams funded by the late Microsoft owner Paul Allen located the wrecks of both the *Doña Paz* and the *Vector*, in around 500 metres of water and both are upright on the seabed. The two ships are less than two miles apart. The footage was kept under wraps until the thirty-second anniversary when it was finally released to commemorate the day when the people of the Philippines suffered what is now known as 'Asia's *Titanic*.'

Chapter 39

Marchioness, 1989

There are few shipwrecks in the world that include the security of being so close to land, and even fewer that have led to any major death tolls. With the capsizing of the *Eastland* in Chicago in 1915 while still tied up to the jetty, a casualty list of over 800 killed made this one of the worst, but most unlikely, disasters in history.

So, one would think that the River Thames in London would be one of the safest places to travel by boat, especially with the number of landmarks that keep the skipper of any vessel aware of where he is going. In 1878, the paddle steamer *Princess Alice* and the collier *Bywell Castle* collided on this very river: the sinking steamer cost the lives of over 600 passengers, making her the worst inland shipping disaster in UK history. But surely something as unique as this couldn't happen again?

Fast forward to 1989 and we are in the centre of London, a city that always seems to be racing to a whole new level.

On the Thames sat the pleasure boats, small vessels popular with the tourists and some which had seen action during the Second World War at Dunkirk. One of these Dunkirk veterans was the 66-year-old *Marchioness*, an 85-foot-long party boat that could carry over 100 people and was regularly hired out for private events for a memorable cruise up and down the river where her passengers could enjoy two decks to roam, dance and drink with friends. Since she was first built in 1923, the vessel had gone through several realms of ownership and reconstruction, the addition of more decking and licensing for the serving of alcohol, as well as any safety features that were required by law.

In the early morning hours of 20 August 1989, she was alongside Embankment Pier taking on members of a party to celebrate the birthday of banker Antonio de Vasconcellos who planned to celebrate his 26th birthday going up and down the river until dawn. When everybody was deemed to be on board, and with around 130 people now making sure that the party was in full swing, the *Marchioness* slipped her mooring and headed downriver towards Tower Bridge.

At around the same time and heading in the same direction was the *Bowbelle*, a 25-year-old dredger that was 262 feet long and so much bulkier than the smaller *Marchioness*. With Captain Douglas Henderson in charge, he had set off from further up the Thames at Battersea loaded with aggregate and was now heading downstream. At 0146 hours, as the pleasure cruiser was making her way under Southwark Bridge, the larger vessel banged into the stern and forced the cruiser to port, leaving the entire side of the vessel at the mercy of the dredger's bow.

In less than thirty seconds the *Bowbelle* had crunched into the *Marchioness* and pushed it underwater, ripping off the upper decks as it went. Dozens of people now found themselves underwater and fighting for their lives, the wall at the edge of river so close yet so far. The dredger carried on forward until hitting Cannon Street Bridge and coming to a stop.

The *Hurlingham*, sister vessel to the *Marchioness*, was nearby and had been already overtaken by the *Bowbelle*, so was first on the scene to pull survivors out of the freezing-cold water. Wreckage from the cruiser littered the water as by now she was completely sunk, trapping partygoers within her hull.

Emergency services were quickly on the scene and survivors were rushed to hospital suffering from shock, cold, injuries and near drowning. None of the life-preserving facilities had had the chance to be used as the collision and sinking were so quick to even think.

The following morning, as dawn broke, the full horror of the disaster became apparent. Fifty-one people had been killed, and several of these would not be found until later when their bodies drifted downstream. One of those who died was Antonio de Vasconcellos, the host of the party.

For the families of those who died, the trauma was only just beginning. A series of high-profile court cases put the disaster into the headlines, starting with the inquest. As part of the identification process it was found that twenty-five victims had had their hands cut off and removed, which not only shocked the grieving loved ones but led to an outcry within the media over the methods adopted and the lack of sympathy.

Several family members started the Marchioness Action Group to push for justice. At one point the coroner openly described one of the mothers as 'unhinged', which also caused an outcry. The inquests were delayed indefinitely and it was only the hard work of the MAG that allowed a new coroner to reopen the inquests and eventually a verdict of unlawful killing was passed.

In April 1990, the captain of the *Bowbelle* went on trial, charged with failing to keep an effective lookout but the jury failed to reach a verdict, the same with a retrial later on in the year. A later private prosecution against the owners was thrown out due to insufficient evidence.

The inquiries pinpointed the cause of the disaster and blamed both ships for failing to keep a proper lookout, stating that visibility from both vessels was severely restricted with both heading in the same direction under the same archway of the same bridge. The Marine Accident Investigation Branch report was heavily criticized for not interviewing anyone on either ship and instead relying on police reports to form their conclusions.

A fight to hold a further public inquiry was successful and, in March 2001, a report was published that blamed both vessels for not keeping a proper lookout and said that the captain of the *Bowbelle*, along with the forward lookout, had been in the pub drinking lager together in the hours before sailing the vessel out that evening, a factor that was highlighted with much criticism from the chair, Lord Justice Clarke. The *Bowbelle* captain was also criticized for not rendering proper assistance, knowing that his ship had just run down another vessel and did not deploy any life-saving aids to survivors in the water.

Today a memorial adorns the floor in Southward Cathedral, as well as several smaller plaques along the Thames near where the collision happened. A permanent lifeboat station run by the Royal National Lifeboat Institute was opened in 2002 at Victoria Embankment, a more positive legacy of a truly terrible event.

The dredger *Bowbelle* was later sold off and renamed *Bom Rei*. In 1996 she broke in two and sank off Madeira, killing one crewmember. The wreck is today a popular dive site and has been visited by tourists and explorers alike. The wreck of the *Marchioness* was raised by a salvage barge and taken away to be later broken up, a sad end to a fine vessel that had played such a heroic role five decades previously.

Chapter 40

Oceanos, 1991

In many stories of disaster at sea you will be able to identify who are the heroes and who are the villains, almost like a film set up to persuade the viewer which party to cheer on while the ship is sinking. But in the loss of the cruise liner *Oceanos*, there were more heroes than normal when something extraordinary happened.

The 14,000-gross-ton liner was launched in 1952 and went through a host of name changes and different owners over the next two decades before finally being acquired by Greek shipping company Epirotiki Lines, and named the *Oceanos*. At 502 feet long, with her cream-coloured hull and single blue funnel with the company logo in yellow, she was an old ship by the time passengers boarded her on 3 August 1991 at the South African port of East London, bound for Durban.

Before she had even got out to sea, the ship was straight into bad weather, with most passengers heading to their cabins or sitting indoors and enjoying the night's entertainment. Throughout the evening the ship pitched and rolled heavily as the waves smashed against her side, the occupants being quite uncomfortable when transiting between decks or trying to get some rest. The service in the restaurant was even worse with the staff barely able to serve the food. Anything that was not secured was sliding off tables or falling onto the deck; this was going to be a very rough night.

On board the ship were 571 passengers and crew. The entertainers were on stage, giving their usual performance – the show had to continue as long as an audience was there. Moss and Tracey Hills were a husband-and-wife team who have always had a love of the sea, along with Julian Butler and Robin Boltman who performed to the delight of the passengers despite the struggle to stay upright.

At around 2130 hours, a slight explosion was heard and the ship's power died. With nobody having a clue what was going, on the entertainment continued. It was at this point that a clear disturbance was seen outside. Taking his video camera with him, Moss Hills went to have a look. What he saw shocked him: the lifeboats were being launched by the crew who were casually boarding them with their belongings before being lowered into the stormy sea. Confused as to why they were doing this, he went down below, but seeing nothing, he returned soon after; however, the sight of water flooding the lower decks stopped him in his tracks. As he filmed the seawater sloshing around and getting higher, he simply said, 'Well, I guess we're going down.'

By the time he had got back up to the lounge to tell his colleagues, most of the crew had evacuated the ship and deserted the passengers on a sinking liner in the middle of a storm. The last few boats were about to leave and Moss and his team got as many passengers into them as possible before the crew launched the last one, half full.

It was now the early morning of 4 August and several of the entertainers headed to the bridge after ordering all passengers onto the upper deck. The bridge was deserted and so they took turns on the radio, transmitting 'Mayday' to anybody who was out there. A cargo ship, *Nedlloyd Mauritius*, picked up the call and asked questions about the ship that Moss Hills couldn't possibly answer. When he was asked what rank he was, the nonplussed radio operator heard, 'I'm a guitarist.'

Still on board the ship were the captain, Yiannis Avranas, and a few officers sitting near the pool while the entertainers conducted the rescue operation. By now the shore authorities had been alerted and South African Air Force helicopters were deployed to begin the airlift of over 200 people still on board. Incredibly, the captain was in the second helicopter off, three hours after he had estimated that the ship had between two and three hours left to live. Although Moss was disgusted with his behaviour, he now had a job to do. He had the full attention of everybody on board who were now huddled on the ever-sloping decks wearing lifejackets.

Against all odds, by early afternoon every single person who was on board the *Oceanos* had been rescued, Moss and Tracey Hills, Julian Butler and Robin Boltman successfully coordinating what was one of the most astounding life-saving airlifts in history with all 571 survivors now on their way to safety.

At around 1530 that afternoon, the *Oceanos* rolled further over until her entire bow was underwater, the stern rising up into the air and everything left on the upper deck free falling into the sea. Fifteen minutes later the name on her stern slipped beneath the waves and she was gone.

When the celebrations of the rescue were over, the anger towards the crew and the company were quick to follow. In what amounted to feeble excuses as to why a captain and his crew should leave their passengers to fend for themselves, Avranas simply justified it with the following statement: 'When I order abandon the ship it doesn't matter what time I leave; abandon is for everybody. If some people like to stay, they can stay.'

Needless to say, this didn't go down well and both Avranas and his crew were convicted of negligence by a Greek court. As for Moss, Tracey, Robin and Julian, they were highly praised and left the scene as the heroes of the story. Amazingly, this would not be the last time these people were involved in a shipwreck, but more on that in chapter 43.

Today the wreck of the *Oceanos* is in a maximum of 97 metres of water and resting on her starboard side. She was dived just a week after the sinking by a news channel team who reported the difficulty with the conditions that only allowed them a few minutes on site at the most. As more people have launched expeditions to her over the years, it became apparent that this is one of the most difficult wreck dives in the world and one that requires a lot of consideration before attempting to dive her.

With her name still on her stern, the bridge area has since collapsed but she still presents an awesome sight for those brave enough to visit her resting place. But the most fascinating part of this story is the exhausting efforts of a few people who stepped up to the mark when the going got tough. These people will forever be known as the heroes of the *Oceanos*.

Chapter 41

Braer, 1993

A t the northernmost tip of Scotland lie two island chains that follow on from each other and have been considered one of those 'out of the way' places for as long as anybody can remember. The Orkney Islands were always famous for being the home to the Royal Navy during two world wars, but the Shetland Islands comprise mostly sheep farming and fishing with no major port to accommodate a fleet of warships like its nearby rival.

But in 1993 this northernmost archipelago became the focus of a major environmental disaster that started with a chain reaction of events in Norway just days before. Loading up for a transatlantic voyage was the Liberian-registered oil tanker *Braer*, 792 feet long and just under 45,000 gross tons. Built in Nagasaki, Japan, in 1975, she could travel along at a speed of around 14.5 knots.

Setting sail from the port of Mongstad in Norway on 3 January 1993, the *Braer* was bound for Quebec, Canada, with a cargo of 84,700 tonnes of light crude oil and a crew of thirty-four, but as soon as she left the safety of the harbour, she almost instantly met with rough seas and heavy storms as she made her way to the usual route of the North Fair Isle Strait.

But the following evening there were major problems on board. Routine boiler adjustments had led to difficulties reigniting it and several pieces of pipework had broken loose on the upper deck. If that wasn't bad enough, it was discovered that seawater had contaminated the diesel oil and attempts were now being made to drain it down and recommence the supply to the engine and generator.

At 0440 hours on 5 January, the ship's engines failed, along with the generator, leaving the *Braer* now drifting ten miles from the Shetland Islands and still in a ferocious storm. The captain placed a call out for towing assistance and the coastguard was informed, but as it became apparent that the ship could not restart, the crew prepared to abandon ship.

As the morning wore on, the *Braer* got closer to land despite all attempts by local tugs in securing a line in what were impossible conditions. The last of the crew was winched to safety and the ship was left to drift onto the rocks. Salvage teams finally managed to board her but were still unable to get a line across. The ship finally ran aground at an area known as Garths Ness at 1119 hours.

From the minute the ship hit the rocks, the sea around her began to turn black as her cargo of thick crude oil leaked into the sea. Being so close to land, it was not long before this started to wash ashore with the stormy seas smashing the treacle-like waves onto the cliffs and beaches. Already a major disaster was in the making while the salvage teams struggled to get the tanker off the rocks. With echoes of the *Torrey Canyon* in the back of their minds, the race was on to prevent the oil spill from destroying an area of natural beauty.

The coast around where the *Braer* had come to grief was a haven for birds and seals; it was not uncommon to see birdwatchers lining up to get a glimpse of an Atlantic puffin, great skua or a storm-petrel. The Shetland Islands offered a wealth of animals across many different species and breeds that gave it its unique appearance and unrivalled features.

Over the next few days hundreds of people volunteered to help with the clean-up operation: from scrubbing and hosing down the rocks, cleaning the beaches and helping the Royal Society for the Protection of Birds (RSPB) gather in all the animals to be cleaned up. More and more organizations swung into action and donations came in thick and fast with people all over the UK sending in blankets, towels, detergent, washing-up liquid and anything that could be used to save the lives of the stricken creatures.

But still, hundreds of dead birds washed ashore, their wings unable to cope with the weight of the sticky black glue-like substance rendering the feathers useless. Many choked on what they had swallowed and were simply collected in black bags and disposed of. With each tide, it seemed that the clean-up operation was a waste of time. The *Braer* sat on the rocks, day after day, her huge bulk awash with stormy seawater that quickly turned black with every wave that crashed over her. The distinctive orange funnel with a huge letter M at the top was the image that most newspapers flashed on their front pages day after day. Salvage tugs from the Dutch company Smit stood by helpless as strong winds and heavy seas tossed the smaller vessels around like bath toys. All they could do was wait for the opportunity.

But, on 12 January 1993, after a week of trying to save the ship from sinking, the *Braer* could finally take no more and broke up on the rocks. This was now officially her entire cargo of oil gone into the sea over the space of seven days. There was now nothing more to be done but clean up the huge mess that would remain a part of the Shetland coast for years to come.

Incredibly, the storm had actually forced much of the oil out to sea. The oil itself was a variety known as Gulfaks crude that was actually lighter than most and more easily biodegradable, making this less of a disaster than it potentially could have been.

This offered no consolation to those affected by the spill though, as the final toll was around 1,500 seabirds dead as well as the distress caused to the grey seals that became very ill because of the oil. The populations of sea animals would take many years to recover.

An inquiry would later blame storm damage as well as some of the actions of the master and crew, but a later news article by an author of a book on the sinking would claim that recently available documents revealed that the *Braer* was in a shocking state of neglect and the sinking was due to a host of failures and bad maintenance: the ship was unseaworthy, a disaster waiting to happen.

Today the wreck of the *Braer* is lying where she grounded, her bow still sticking up out of the water as a permanent marker of what went so drastically wrong in what should have been a simple journey across the sea. But it soon became apparent that once again lessons were not learned quickly enough.

Chapter 42

Estonia, 1994

Since the *Princess Victoria* and the *Herald of Free Enterprise* disasters, the flaws in the design of the roll-on/roll-off ferries have always been that elephant in the room but it was not something that could be helped without changing the design so drastically that it would no longer be a car ferry in the truest sense.

Yet, another major ferry disaster would hit the front pages that would shock Europe, least of all for the suddenness of the sinking and the staggering death toll.

The car ferry *Estonia* was built in 1980 at the Meyer Werft shipyard in Papenburg which at the time was in West Germany, and launched on 26 April that year. At 509 feet 11 inches (later being lengthened to 515 feet), she was 15,598 gross tons with space for around 2,000 passengers and up to 460 cars on her two car decks. Over the next fourteen years she went through various changes of owner as well as names, first being launched as the *Viking Sally* (Viking Line), *Silja Star* (Silja Line), *Wasa King* (Wasa Line) and finally the *Estonia* in 1993 (Estline).

Her main route was Tallinn, Estonia, to Stockholm, Sweden, but she had been known to make the Helsinki route over to Finland. Upon the collapse of the Soviet Union, the ship became the largest Estonian-owned vessel at the time.

On Tuesday, 27 September 1994, the ship was at her regular terminal in the port of Tallinn, loading up with passengers and vehicles and preparing to make the overnight journey to Stockholm, a trip she had conducted hundreds of times over the years. In the Baltic Sea a storm was brewing but nothing too drastic; she had encountered the worst that Mother Nature had thrown at her in the past so this should prove no different to any others.

With 803 passengers and 186 crew on board, she headed out of the ferry terminal and westward to Sweden. On board her passengers settled down in the cabins and lounges, many of them dozing in the seating areas or enjoying a few drinks.

At around 0100 hours on 28 September, a loud bang was heard at the bow, caused by heavy waves striking the underside of the door. On many of these ships there are two bow doors: the first one is the bow itself that lifts up on hinges, known as the visor, which reveals a second door behind it which is lowered to also act as a loading ramp for cars. What they couldn't see on the bridge was that waves were constantly battering the door and although there was no indication of trouble, this continued for several minutes.

Suddenly, at 0115 hours, the entire bow door fell off and was swallowed by the waves which in turn exposed the second door and car deck to the sea. Instantly the *Estonia* was in major trouble as the door was not designed to hold back the sea to such an extent. The ship took on an immediate list and a Mayday call was sent out to all ships in the area. Other ferries from both Silja Line and Viking Line turned towards her position and sped to render assistance as search and rescue centres in Sweden, Estonia and Finland were notified of the ferry in trouble in the middle of the Baltic.

By 0130 hours the ship had listed to starboard and stayed over at around 60 degrees, the alarms on board already alerting everybody to an emergency. By now the significant rolling of the ship left everybody on board without any doubt that the ship was in significant danger. Water flooded in further as each wave and swell smashed against the ship, the list intensified as life rafts were launched. There was no chance to get the lifeboats out, as with the state of the list, they were rendered useless.

Several ferries were in constant communications with the ship with the *Silja Europa* and the *Mariella* asking for more information. *Estonia* repeated her position and then told them that she had suffered a blackout. After that there was no further word from her.

By now people were scrambling onto the side of the ship and sliding into the sea with lifejackets on: the freezing water meant that survival was measured in minutes. With the ship now completely on her side, she rolled over and sank stern first, leaving a sea of orange survival equipment floating on the surface.

The *Mariella* was first on the scene around half an hour after the sinking; she picked up fifteen survivors from life rafts and was then used as the main helicopter support ship for coordinating the rescue operation as the air rescue services were coming in from all angles.

When morning came, only 137 people were found to have survived the sinking. The final death toll was put at 852, making her the worst European peacetime disaster in history. The shock of the sinking of such a modern ship led to an immediate investigation into what went wrong. The wreck of the *Estonia* was located within days at a depth of up to 279 feet of water and resting on her starboard side. Images of her name in ghostly video footage were broadcast to the world as hundreds of victims were still on board. (A later mission to cover the ship in concrete got as far as dumping pebbles over the wreck.) Today the ship is still in the same spot being monitored by Finland for divers who disobey the rules that prohibit visiting her.

An investigation in 1997 concluded that the locking pins on the bow door failed in the storm and the stormy waves eventually ripped the visor off, letting the water onto the car deck. The bow door was found around a mile away from the wreck and recovered by a salvage ship for the investigators to examine.

Today memorials exist in both Stockholm and Tallinn, the two cities that lost more than any other country. In Sweden a circular wall names the victims just over the road from the wreck of the *Vasa* in her museum; in Tallinn a piece of art known as the Broken Line commemorates the dead near the terminal from where she sailed all those years ago.

In 2020 a team of investigative reporters released a video that showed a hole in the wreck that they claimed helped sink the ship, although this was soon discounted by officials. In any case, the hole was only a few feet long and the wreck had been on the seabed over 25 years by then, the hole most likely caused by the vessel hitting the seabed or general corrosion.

While the sinking of the *Estonia* is now confined to the history books and the museums, the ship herself threw out a reminder of what happened when, in 2017, a team of forestry administration personnel were investigating a rose bush in Finland and found a crushed life ring bearing the name of the lost ferry. The crushed Styrofoam meant that the life-saving device had to have been under extreme pressure, which could only have come from being on the wreck itself.

While conspiracy theorists still put forward their own causes of the disaster and other families of victims demand the salvage, the *Estonia* will most likely remain where she is, protected from the elements and salvors and forever a grave of the victims of Europe's worst ferry disaster.

Chapter 43

Achille Lauro, 1994

There are many ships that have suffered a tragic ending, some experiencing more than one incident during their service that has thrust them into the realms of being unlucky, but none has had a history quite like that of the liner *Achille Lauro*.

Launched on 1 July 1946 by Queen Wilhelmina of Holland, the Dutch liner started her career as the 21,119-gross-ton *Willem Ruys*, a ship 642 feet in length with two short funnels gracing her grey-coloured hull. Her building had been delayed by the Second World War but once she was launched, her career began with a service between the Netherlands and the East Indies.

Another Dutch liner, the *Oranje*, was both her rival and running mate, and in 1953 the *Oranje* and the *Willem Ruys* collided in the Red Sea, both suffering minor damage. If that wasn't bad enough, just months later a second collision involving the *Willem Ruys*, this time with the tanker *Cornelis B*, sank the latter and her crew of eight were taken on board the *Willem Ruys*.

The ship went several years without another incident but due to a decline in passenger numbers, the ship was berthed in Rotterdam and sold to Italian cruise line Flotta Lauro in 1965 who renamed the ship *Achille Lauro* after the founder of the company. But as the ship was undergoing reconstruction work in Palermo in August that year, an explosion tore into the ship, causing damage. Not a good start to a career with the new owners, but she was soon repaired and out at sea with paying passengers once again. By now she was painted a dark blue with tall funnels, each carrying a white star.

On 19 May 1972, she suffered another fire whilst alongside Genoa, which left structural damage. In October that year, the crew went on strike while in the Canary Islands, which left 1,400 passengers stranded for a week. Three years later, on 28 April 1975, she was in collision yet again, this time sinking the cargo ship *Youssef.* By now the ship had been in more incidents than most other ships, yet, incredibly, she was still a popular vessel to holiday on and she was well loved by an army of admirers.

But, on 2 December 1981, while cruising off the Canary Islands, a fire on board left three of her passengers dead. This was the worst incident yet and within two months she was impounded in Tenerife for non-payment of debts by her owners. This was both tragic and embarrassing for the people who ran the ship, as well as frustrating for her crew, but nothing would prepare them for what happened a few years later during a Mediterranean cruise.

On 7 October 1985, four Arab terrorists from the Palestine Liberation Front entered the dining room and fired automatic weapons into the air, causing panic amongst the passengers. The captain was forced onto the bridge and told to turn the ship about, to Syria. The *Achille Lauro* had been hijacked. For the next two days the ship was in a state of terror as the four hijackers tormented the terrified hostages. Due to shore excursions in Egypt, there were only 97 passengers on board and 450 crew, but this was enough to grab the world's attention.

The following day, the hijackers collected the passports of those on board; they wanted to know who was Jewish and American and began separating people into groups. They beat some of the passengers for being Jewish and demanded the release of fifty Palestinian prisoners from Israeli prisons. If their demands were not met, they would start killing the hostages, they said. When their demands were not met, they took the wheelchair-bound Leon Klinghoffer and shot him dead before throwing his body overboard.

The following day the *Achille Lauro* was anchored off Port Said, Egypt, where safe passage was given to the hijackers in return for the hostages. As the hijackers fled, their plane was later intercepted and forced to land in Italy, sparking a diplomatic incident. But with the hijackers now jailed, the liner was free to proceed

This attack on innocent people on a cruise thrust the liner into the history books and became synonymous with terrorism, leading to several books, films and even an opera. In the meantime, the *Achille Lauro* went back to cruising, her reputation now cemented.

The owners were rebranded in 1987 as StarLauro and it was under this company when she was on a cruise in the Indian Ocean, on 30 November

1994. With 979 passengers and crew on board, she was just off the coast of Somalia when fire broke out in the early hours of the morning. With the danger of it spreading, although it seemed contained within the engine spaces, the order was given to evacuate the passengers, and the lifeboats were filled up and launched.

A distress signal was sent out and several ships in the area responded, including the warships USS *Halyburton* and USS *Gettysburg*, as well as the tanker *Hawaiian King* which was first on the scene. By the time daylight broke, the ship was emitting smoke from the side of the hull. Lifeboats were dotted around the sea waiting their turn to be picked up. In the evacuation two people were killed and eight injured. But the amazing thing at this point was that among the survivors were entertainers Julian Butler, Robin Boltman and Moss and Tracey Hills who had coordinated the *Oceanos* rescue three years before. Once again, their presence gave the papers a good story although, on this occasion, the evacuation was more organized and they were merely survivors of the disaster.

The passengers and crew boarded the various cargo ships and warships now on scene and headed to Djibouti to be landed and flown back to their respective countries. Despite the two deaths, the rescue had been an enormous success and the survivors made lifelong friends with the crew of these vessels.

For two days the *Achille Lauro* burned in the Indian Ocean, the side of the ship charred and smoking, visible for miles. She drifted with the tides, ships standing by in case the burning liner required a tow away from other ships. Tugs were on hand on the off chance that the ship burned itself out and could be brought back to port, but this was not meant to be as, on 2 December 1994, the ship finally sank. With such a varied life, after forty-seven years, the story of the *Achille Lauro* was now officially at an end. Her wreck has never been located.

With an incredible tale such as this, it is only amazing that more books have not been written about this beloved yet unlucky liner, but thankfully, with the number of fans this ship had – and still has – the thousands of happy memories made on her will continue to live forever.

Chapter 44

Maria Asumpta, 1995

There have been few ships from the 1800s that have been preserved for posterity but there are even fewer that still sail: century-old ships tend to suffer from rot and general wear and tear until the ship is no longer in its original state. But one ship did continue to sail the seas, for 137 years.

The brig *Maria Asumpta* was launched in Badalona, Spain, in 1858 and sailed across the Atlantic on many occasions, with slaves and general cargo to Argentina. At 123 feet long, she weighed just 127 tons. She was rigged with an engine in the 1930s, which assisted her two masts when the wind was not strong enough.

Around this time, she was renamed *Pepita* and her rigging was reduced, later being renamed yet again in 1953 when she became the *Ciudad de Inca*. But she was showing her age, her masts had been removed and by 1978, the brig was only working in the Mediterranean. The owners at the time saw no further use for her and planned to set her on fire at sea, so the China Clipper Society purchased her for the price of her engines. The two founders, Mark Litchfield and Robin Cecil-Wright, set about restoring her to her former glory. By 1982, she was once again back at sea and used for training purposes, even taking part in a tall ships event two years later on Lake Ontario.

But tragedy struck when the sailing vessel *Marques*, also owned by Litchfield and Cecil-Wright, sank in a gale on 2 June 1984, with the loss of nineteen lives. There were just nine survivors. Because of this, the owners were engaged in a lawsuit that prevented the *Ciudad de Inca* leaving her berth and she remained on the Great Lakes for several years until she sank in the winter of 1986.

Thankfully, it was only in shallow water and she was quickly raised and restored again. By 1988 the owners had renamed her back to her original name – *Maria Asumpta* – and she was no longer classed as a sail training ship but came under the category of a private yacht.

She was now 130 years old and officially the oldest commercial sailing ship in the world. She later regained her title as sail training vessel where she once again was allowed to participate in tall ships events. She was also involved in filming opportunities, amongst them the 1995 miniseries *Buffalo Girls*, as well as *The Master of Ballantrae*, a film based on the Robert Louis Stevenson novel.

Mark Litchfield, an ex-Royal Navy officer, was in command of the *Maria Asumpta* on 30 May 1995 as she was transiting the coast of Cornwall following a refit. The journey from Gloucester had been one that caused her to shelter several times in three different ports and now she was bound for Padstow harbour where she would tie up once again. Litchfield was taking a route that brought her between The Mouls and Pentire Point, a route that was not recommended by the Admiralty, but he wanted to 'enjoy the view'. This was a decision that would come back to haunt him.

The ship's engines suddenly failed and, with the tidal currents, the *Maria Asumpta* was now at the mercy of the Cornish sea heading towards the rocks. Just minutes later the bottom of the ship hit Rump Point and holed the ship, and water began flooding into the lower decks. A Mayday call was quickly sent and it was soon evident that the ship could not survive.

People on shore watched the ship from sailing by to a ship in distress and, within minutes of striking the rocks, the crew began to abandon ship. Some jumped onto the rocks themselves and climbed away from the ship, but several were left on board. Five people were pulled out of the sea by a fishing vessel that had come in close. Another six were airlifted from the cliffs and rushed to hospital, but three others were missing. Litchfield was one of those who survived after being rescued from the rocks. Two life rafts inflated and anchored themselves to the wreck as the waves battered the ship but very soon the ageing ship began to break up.

Photographs taken from the top of the cliffs show the ship heeling over to starboard and her rigging almost touching the tips of the waves, her hull being smashed up with every surge of the waves against the rocks. Pieces of her broke off and floated nearby, reminding the viewer that she was only made of wood. As the search continued for the three missing crew, the ship became nothing more than a floating collection of splintered planks, a sad end to such a long and distinguished career. The body of one of those missing was soon found.

On 14 February 1996, Mark Litchfield was charged with the manslaughter of the three victims and went on trial a year later. Pleading not guilty, he was faced with overwhelming evidence that he had acted dangerously and negligently. He had not only been warned of those rocks, but he had been faced with concerns regarding the state of the engines, just before they failed for the final time. More damning, it was highlighted that he fled to safety, leaving three of his fellow crewmembers to die. With eyewitness and expert testimony, he didn't have a leg to stand on and the jury found him guilty of manslaughter on 7 August 1997, jailing him for eighteen months.

The sinking of the *Maria Asumpta* was a sad event, both in terms of lives lost and the loss of such a historic vessel, when the whole event could have been avoided with a touch of common sense and care. A memorial to the three who died that day is in St Enodoc Church in the Cornish village of Trebetherick, not far from where the ship went down, after 137 years of sailing the seas.

Chapter 45

Kursk, 2000

In any seagoing adventure or voyage, one aspect is, without doubt, one of the most dangerous occupations of them all – the submariner. Being enclosed in a metal compartment and then diving underwater hundreds of feet is not for the faint-hearted, but we have been doing this for over a hundred years, ever since it became the norm to send them to sea armed with torpedoes and tinned food. Incredibly, the loss of a submarine these days is rare, but when they do meet with disaster, it sends a shockwave round the world.

The Oscar II class of Russian nuclear submarine is one of the largest submarines in the world, displacing over 12,000 tons, with a length of 508 feet 6 inches and width of 59 feet 9 inches, making the Oscar II a formidable sight to behold. One of the fourteen that were completed was the *Kursk*, designated K-141, which was launched in 1994 and powered by two nuclear reactors which pushed her two propellers silently at around 32 knots underwater – more than what some surface ships are able to achieve. She carried a crew of 118.

Despite the pride of the Russians in their submarine fleet, the *Kursk* only completed one deployment during her lifetime, a six-month trip to the Mediterranean; the rest of the time she was in port or not far away from her home base of Vidyayevo in Russia. On 10 August 2000, she joined a large exercise named Summer-X, which involved over two dozen warships and four submarines. As the exercise kicked off, *Kursk* successfully launched a missile with a dummy warhead and two days later prepared to do the same with a torpedo. So far it was progressing well. But hundreds of miles away, something didn't seem right.

At 0729 GMT, a Norwegian seismic detection system recorded a small event on their equipment in the middle of the Russian exercise, followed just over two minutes later by a second one, this one measuring 4.2 on the Richter Scale. This set alarm bells ringing on both sides of the Atlantic.

Meanwhile, in the Barents Sea the expected torpedo firing had not gone ahead yet explosions were detected. Confusion reigned amongst the fleet and reports were sent to their shore authorities when the *Kursk* was no longer answering their transmissions. It would be several hours before the required communications check that it was assumed that disaster had befallen the submarine.

At 1830 GMT the exercise was stopped as the Northern Fleet declared an emergency: the search for the submarine became the top priority. But the world would not be told about this, for even twenty-four hours after the emergency had been declared the exercise was still being described as a resounding success. The heads of the Russian navy knew differently as they frantically searched for their comrades.

It would be forty-eight hours after the *Kursk* had vanished that a press conference announced that the submarine had experienced difficulties, still downplaying the magnitude of the disaster. But by now it was obvious what had gone on as more information filtered out – the submarine had sunk two days earlier.

As the submarine was located and attempts were made to make contact with any survivors, incredibly, offers of help from both the British and Norwegians was declined. It would be five days after the loss that the Russian authorities finally accepted this and teams of their divers arrived on scene, but by now it was six days too late.

Over the coming days the *Kursk* was dived on and the damage to the vessel was clear to see – her bow was a complete mess, her demise an obvious case of a major incident forward which the Russians at first blamed on a collision with a foreign submarine despite a complete lack of any evidence.

As the divers slowly made their way inside the wreck, it was clear to see that the entire crew of the *Kursk* had died in the disaster, making this one of the world's worst ever submarine losses. The families of those who died began to get restless at the lack of information and accusations grew that the navy was involved in a cover-up. One woman was filmed shouting at one of these meetings before being injected with a sedative which made her stop shouting and collapse in the arms of the person next to her. This image spoke volumes about the catastrophic handling of the case as well as the way the families were being treated.

While the fallout from the sinking was being handled on shore, the operation to raise the *Kursk* had to be carried out. With two nuclear reactors on board, as well as explosives, bodies, secrets and unanswered questions, plans were put in place to bring the submarine back home. First the salvage crews used a thick cable attached to a mechanism on a support ship so that it acted much like a giant cheese wire, cutting backwards and forwards at the bow until it had sliced the damaged front end completely off. Now they could concentrate on the more stable section, which in this case was 90 per cent of the submarine.

The wreck was attached to a set of hoisting cables and a huge salvage barge directly above slowly pulled the submarine from her resting place and held her suspended just below the barge, towing the wrecked vessel all the way from the site of her sinking to the naval base at Murmansk.

In mid-October 2001, when she finally got to her destination, the vessel was lowered into a dry dock and the barge sailed out from above her. When the salvors were happy that she was stable, the dry dock was pumped dry and the *Kursk* once again revealed her conning tower to the world's press, her shield still showing the red and yellow which had come to be her identity.

When the investigators went on board, they located many of the bodies of those who had died, but it was then that the full horror of what had happened was revealed. One officer had written a note in the dark, explaining what had happened and that he was trapped alive with twenty-two other men. As the hours ticked by, they most likely died of extreme cold while trapped in the aft compartments, leading to many people believing that they could have been rescued if only the Russian navy had swallowed their pride and asked for help straight away.

The sinking of the *Kursk* has inspired many books and even a big-budget film was released in 2019 starring Colin Firth. As the wreck of the submarine was broken up for scrap, her conning tower was saved and turned into a memorial itself in Murmansk, a permanent reminder of a dark chapter in Russian naval history.

When the cause of the accident was eventually discovered, it came as a shock to many. Her torpedoes contained High Test Peroxide (HTP), a cheap but powerful chemical. It was thought that a leak of HTP had caused the explosion in the bow which two minutes later set off a second explosion of kerosene that was used as torpedo fuel. Most navies had stopped using HTP decades before, after HMS *Sidon* had suffered a similar accident in 1955 that led to the deaths of thirteen crew.

But despite the chaos of the whole incident and the inability to ask for help, lessons were learned and this was proved five years later. The mini-submarine *AS-28 Priz* got into difficulties off the coast of Kamchatka and became trapped on the seafloor 600 feet down with seven crew on board. Russia appealed for assistance and immediately got a response from Britain, America and Japan, and forty-eight hours later the crew were saved and the submarine brought to the surface. This became a public image of what can be achieved when rival navies work together to get a job done.

Chapter 46

Le Joola, 2002

In 2002 we once again find ourselves confronted with the loss of another RORO ferry, this time in the African country of Senegal. Since the loss of the *Estonia* there had been countless incidents and disasters involving the same type of ferry, including the *Express Samina* off Greece when, on 26 September 2000, the crew were not paying attention and the ship struck a huge rock with a light on top warning of danger. Ninety people were killed in the disaster, but it seemed that this particular date was destined as a symbol of tragedy as exactly two years later, thousands of miles away on the west coast of Africa, another tragedy unfolded.

Built in Germany and launched in March 1990, *Le Joola* was a small ferry of just 259 feet 2 inches in length with a gross tonnage of 2,087 tons. This was a standard roll-on/roll-off vessel, owned and operated by the government of Senegal, with a full-load capacity of 536 passengers, 44 crew and 35 cars. The ferry often made the trips between Dakar and the Casamance province, transporting locals from one port to another to conduct business and trade market items. She continued on this kind of routine for over ten years before, in September 2001, she was laid up for a year for routine maintenance and replacement of her port engine. She re-entered service on 10 September 2002, and went back to sea carrying her usual complement of passengers.

On the afternoon of 26 September, she set sail from Ziguinchor in Casamance and was clearly overloaded, customary on many of these kinds of ferries. Some estimates put the amount of people on board at around 2,000, almost four times more than what she was licensed to carry. Sailing off into the evening, she was heading towards danger but no one seemed overly concerned.

At 2200 hours that night, the ship reported to a Dakar maritime security centre that all was well, although this changed when just an hour later the ship encountered a storm not far off the Gambian coast. It was probably at this point that the full enormity of the overloading was becoming apparent as the ship was tossed about like a toy.

With a ship that was rumoured to be unseaworthy due to rushed maintenance work and overcrowding, *Le Joola* lurched to one side and rolled over, the ship turning completely upside down. Only a few people managing to get away from the ship as she went over. Dozens of people now found themselves in a stormy sea with nobody knowing what had happened and no way to alert anybody. It would be a miracle if anybody could be seen in this dark and stormy night.

The ferry continued to float upside down, her red hull like a huge marker. The following morning the first rescue teams finally arrived at the wreck, some local fishing boats pulling exhausted survivors out of the water. Those who could get close to the upside-down wreck said they could hear banging from those trapped within the hull. Bad weather was preventing any rescuers being able to get there in time and cut them out of the ship. At 1500 hours on 27 September, the ferry, still full of people, slid beneath the waves, stern first. Only sixty-four survivors were picked up, with only one female, who was pregnant at the time.

Following the sinking, calls for an immediate inquiry mounted and investigators had to try and find out why this ship that had been doing the same journey for over a decade should suddenly capsize and sink. One factor is that she was not supposed to go that far out to sea as her permits only allowed her to sail coastal waters. Further digging revealed that the ship was in a bad state of repair, the owners negligent when it came to keeping the ship maintained to a good standard, despite the state-of-the-art safety equipment on board.

But the one factor that kept cropping up was the overcrowding. How could so many people be allowed on the ship? It was not like the odd few had slipped on board – we are talking over a thousand people extra, many on them on the upper deck which would have left the ship dangerously unstable and top-heavy. These people consisted of over a thousand who actually purchased tickets, others too young to buy tickets (children below the age of 5) and other areas where no checks were carried out with people just somehow ending up on board. The distraught relatives were faced with boards of photographs containing images of bodies laid out, to see if they recognized a brother, sister, son, daughter, mother, father. Very few were initially recovered from the water, although later dives on the wreck located several hundred more. Despite the investigation, no one was ever prosecuted. The true death toll will never be known but it is at least 1,863, making this one of the world's worst peacetime shipwrecks.

The wreck of *Le Joola* was dived on within days of the sinking and over 500 bodies were eventually recovered, many of them never identified. Several memorials were built to commemorate the sinking at the ports where the ship so often called, the hundreds of unknown victims now under one collective name – *Le Joola*.

There have been calls by relatives of those killed to raise the wreck, which lies at a depth of just fifty-nine feet, but so far, the wreck has laid there with no salvage taking place. With this shipwreck comes the knowledge that she is up there as one of the top worst sea disasters of all time, yet the biggest tragedy is that she is one of the most forgotten.

Chapter 47

HMS *Scylla*, 2004

T his shipwreck is not like others: yes, she is a warship, yes, she is British, but the way she met her end was not so much the end, but actually the beginning of a new life for this particular ship. The ship is today known as an artificial reef – a decommissioned ship sunk on purpose to provide a haven for wildlife and sea creatures as well as an attraction to sport divers for the tourism industry.

HMS *Scylla* was a Leander-class frigate built in Devonport Dockyard in Plymouth and launched on 8 August 1968, one of twenty-six of the class that provided the workhorses of the Royal Navy for three decades. The *Scylla* was actually the last warship to be built here and her military career began when she was commissioned on 12 February 1970, under the pennant number F-71.

At 3,251 tons and 372 feet long, she was armed with a twin 4.5-inch gun turret on the bow and Sea Cat missiles when she first joined the fleet. This would change through the years as she would have the newer Sea Wolf and Exocet missiles installed in the 1980s, as well as torpedoes. Her flight deck accommodated both Westland Wasp and Lynx helicopters during her career to support her main role in anti-submarine warfare.

During the 1970s, the Royal Navy was embroiled in the so-called Cod Wars between Britain and Iceland where warships patrolled the waters off Iceland to defend British trawlers against attacks by Icelandic coastguard vessels, one of which collided with *Scylla*.

In May 1976, she escorted the Royal Yacht *Britannia* during Queen Elizabeth II's state visit to Finland before attending the Spithead Fleet Review for the Silver Jubilee.

The 1980s and 1990s saw the frigate take part in several deployments, including hurricane relief operations off the Cayman Islands, Armilla Patrol in the Persian Gulf and South Atlantic operations. On one occasion she collided with the replenishment tanker RFA *Gold Rover* after steering issues caused hull damage to the tanker and superficial damage to the *Scylla*.

By the end of 1993 she was showing her age and was finally decommissioned, to make way for the new Type 23 frigates. She was laid up in Portsmouth, the last of her class, the rest of the Leanders being sold or scrapped, and there she sat for over a decade at anchor in Fareham Creek.

Meanwhile, in the south-west of England, discussions were under way to sink a ship off the coast of Cornwall to create a new attraction. One popular dive site was where the liberty ship *James Egan Layne* had been lost in 1945 in Whitsand Bay; over the years the wreck had been salvaged, dived on and in some of cases divers had died in the wreckage.

With the success of other artificial reefs around the world, such as the USS *Spiegel Grove* which was sunk off Florida in 2002, the hunt was on for the perfect ship to sink for both divers and wildlife, to take the heat off the wartime wrecks and provide a purpose-built safe dive site that would be worth visiting. The *Scylla* was earmarked for the project – a first in Europe if all went ahead okay. A group was put together to make this happen and funding was found to purchase the ship and to make her safe for divers. Enter the National Marine Aquarium.

First the interior was stripped of all things nasty – asbestos, oil, sludge, wiring, anything that could trap a diver or pollute the sea, was removed. Next a series of holes was cut into the hull and superstructure to allow safe access to the interior of the ship. This was different to a ship wrecked by accident: there would be no jagged edges if they could help it and certainly no danger zones if possible. By November 2003 the rusting *Scylla* had been purchased and had been towed out of Portsmouth harbour and into Devonport Dockyard, her birthplace thirty-five years earlier. It was at this point that 120 ex-crewmembers and dockyard workers were allowed a final visit to the ship; this included her last commanding officer, Captain Mike Booth. After saying farewell to their ship, she was prepared for the voyage that would propel her into the history books.

On Saturday, 27 March 2004, just 800 feet from the *James Egan Layne* wreck, the *Scylla* was placed in position and explosive charges laid, the ship was evacuated and cameras set up to record her final journey. With thousands watching from the shore and TV cameras filming, a 12-year-old boy pressed the detonation switch and massive explosions erupted.

In just a few minutes the ship was down by the head and sank out of sight to the cheers of all those who were watching, a new beginning for both the *Scylla* and Whitsand Bay. Once she had settled upright, the divers descended to check that she had landed according to plan and that she was safe for visitors. The news was good.

Over the years the wreck of the *Scylla* has generated a significant amount of revenue for the local tourist industry as thousands of divers explore her hull and internal compartments. Unfortunately, two divers died on her in 2007 after entering the wreck. In 2014, a survey was carried out that highlighted the dangers of her interior and therefore advised visitors to no longer enter the wreck.

Today the wreck is still in good condition, but the interior has deteriorated more than expected and further advice was issued in 2017 declaring the interior of the wreck unsafe for diving and should not be attempted.

Other than that, the wreck of *Scylla* has turned the area into a wildlife haven, a reef for all kinds of sea creatures that would not otherwise have stayed in this area. With this, the history of the *Scylla* takes on a whole new story, one that encompasses a new lease of life for both the ship and the area, while at the same time taking the pressure of nearby historic wrecks. With the success of the sinking of the *Scylla*, it is hoped that more ships will be sunk for this purpose in the near future, the Australians and Americans already sending some of their major ships to the bottom for that reason.

With each new reef vessel on the seabed, the seas are interesting again and that little bit more of a haven for us to enjoy and learn from.

Chapter 48

Al Dana, 2006

For this next shipwreck we come to a style of ship that you very rarely hear about, let alone hearing of one sinking with a large loss of life. But the fate of the *Al Dana* is one of a kind, and the fallout of this tragedy is one that shook a nation. Initially, it was meant as a celebration of a success, a triumph for the engineering world and of pioneering innovation.

The Kingdom of Bahrain is an island nation in the Persian Gulf, one which has slowly been building up to a world-class country of finance and trade. What better way to display this than the building of their World Trade Centre in the capital Manama? Construction began in 2004 with a design that included two identical twin sail-like structures of fifty floors that meet in the middle with three walkways, each one sporting a wind turbine that generates much of the towers' energy in the most sustainable way. By 2006 most of the structure was completed although it still had two more years to go before the official opening, but to celebrate the main job being such a grand success, the construction companies decided to throw a party for their employees to thank them for their hard work.

For this they hired the *Al Dana*, a traditional Arab dhow designed like a traditional trading vessel but had been fitted out as a restaurant vessel for guests. She was licensed as a restaurant and was supposed to remain berthed alongside a jetty, but this did not stop the operators, Island Tours, from sending her out into the bay for what would turn out to be a party cruise. She was a small vessel, only 85 feet long but 25 feet high, not something that would normally cause concern for a vessel like this, but then again, these ships had been sailing the seas for hundreds of years. She was built in the United Arab Emirates in 1996 and had only come over to her new berth at the end of 2005. The vessel had two main decks for passengers. Her single screw could move her slowly and steadily with up to 150 people on board, depending on the party size. She only needed a small crew who would welcome on board the representatives from the construction companies, such as Atkins Consulting and Murray & Roberts, amongst others, who were instrumental in building the skyscraper.

With visible pride, the *Al Dana* welcomed her passengers aboard on the evening of 30 March 2006, promising a night of entertainment and enjoyment. At around 2000 hours the crew slipped the lines and the dhow headed out from her berth into the bay.

At this point many passengers could feel that the boat was swaying even while the jetty was still within sight. Several people had left the vessel before she disembarked, nervous about going aboard, while the rest were asked to head to the lower decks to help distribute the weight evenly.

With the *Al Dana* now in full party mode, the upper deck was being used for dancing when suddenly she began to sway further over than before. The vessel seemed to be doing a U-turn towards the shore which was still only half a mile away. People were now unsteady on their feet and slid down the sloping floors: the ship was now in a situation where she was not righting herself. The entire dhow very quickly fell over onto her starboard side, throwing those on the upper deck into the water and trapping others below decks as the water flooded in without giving anyone a chance to swim to safety.

With so many other boats in the area, it didn't take long for the capsized ship to be spotted. Nearby pleasure boats raced to the scene along with a coastguard vessel, US Marine boats and others within reach. While survivors were being picked up from the water, others climbed onto the port side of the *Al Dana* to pull others out of the capsized hull, breaking windows and dragging them up and into the rescue boats. The US Navy has a permanent base at Manama and quickly mobilized divers and rescue craft to assist the Bahrainis with the search for survivors. But it wasn't long before the bodies of dead passengers were being extracted. A helicopter assisted the search well into the night, but it was clear that this was not going to have a happy ending for what had started out as a celebratory party.

By the following day, it was realized that fifty-eight people had been killed. Questions were already being asked as to why this converted fishing vessel was even allowed to leave her berth when the licence specifically forbade it. An inquiry was launched and immediately the answers were clear to see: the crew and owners had been negligent and put the lives of their passengers at risk by ignoring the rules. The owner of the vessel, Abdulla Al Kobaisi, and the captain, Rajendrakumar Ramjibhai, were put on trial accused of manslaughter. After all the evidence was heard it was apparent that the vessel was clearly unstable with inadequate safety and training procedures. In 2007, the pair were found guilty and sentenced respectively to ten and three years' imprisonment, the owner getting the maximum penalty possible under Bahraini law.

A later civil court judgement ordered Kobaisi to pay each victim 2,000 Bahraini dinars (approximately £3,000) in 2012. Having served more than half his sentence, this was a case of sparing him further jail time on condition that he paid the compensation money.

The sinking of the *Al Dana* is Bahrain's worst sea disaster and a black granite memorial listing all the names today stands in the Old Christian Cemetery in Manama, where each year the families and survivors gather to remember those who went out to celebrate a joyous occasion and tragically never came back.

Chapter 49

Costa Concordia, 2012

The age of the long-distance jet aircraft pretty much made ocean liners obsolete by the late 1960s, and so the big companies running these ships had to completely rebrand: enter the age of the holiday cruise liner. As the next fifty years progressed, these liners got bigger and bigger, each one losing a little of the classic liner charm and becoming more like a water-based hotel with balcony views and water parks for the enjoyment of passengers. One of the companies that operated such ships was Costa Cruises, an Italian operator of dozens of the world's largest liners which had been trading as an ocean-going concern since 1854.

One of the ships in the fleet was the *Costa Concordia*, launched in 2005 and taking her maiden voyage just a year later. With a gross tonnage of 114,147 she was a beast, at 952 feet long and 116 feet wide, room on board for 3,780 passengers and a crew of 1,100 to cater to their every need. Coloured in the standard white hull with a single yellow funnel bearing the company letter C, the ship was a floating maze of entertainment for the people who had booked seven- and fourteen- night cruises around the ports of the world. Sporting a theatre, five spas, gym, pool, sauna, four swimming pools, thirteen bars and a host of other events, venues and activities to make sure that every person who boarded would leave the ship wanting to come back later.

Her career was almost uneventful, save for high winds causing damage to her bow in 2008 when she was pushed against her berth, but which was soon repaired. But this ship was about to become extremely famous for all the wrong reasons.

Captain Francesco Schettino was in charge of the *Costa Concordia* for her voyage out of Civitavecchia on the evening of 13 January 2012, the start of a week-long cruise around the Mediterranean ports. Schettino had been working for Costa for eleven years and was over-confident, bordering almost on reckless. With a woman on the bridge who was not part of the bridge team, in order to show off, he ordered the ship to proceed close to the tiny island of Giglio in order to 'salute' the island.

At 2145 hours the ship found herself too close to land and in an attempt to steer clear of danger, she collided with the rocks, ripping a huge gash in the port side. Water immediately began flooding into the engine room, which very quickly led to a loss of power, steering and propulsion. The ship lurched over to port and drifted closer to shore. By now everyone knew that something was seriously wrong.

Just twenty-four minutes later, the ship, drifting in the wind, grounded almost at the harbour of Giglio, slowly listing further over, this time to starboard. It was over an hour after the collision that the order to abandon ship was given and the lifeboats lowered. Being so close to shore, it was a relatively easy rescue effort and so there was a good chance that everybody might get off alive.

A massive rescue operation was now under way. She had set sail with 3,206 passengers and 1,023 crew, and it looked like the small village nearby was going to be very crowded as boats began dropping off their human cargo and shuttling back out to the ship. There was chaos and confusion with the Guardia di Finanza (local law enforcement) boat making calls to the ship that went unanswered.

Helicopters now swarmed the area among the local boats. Hundreds of people were being pulled out of the water but it was apparent that several people had died during the evacuation, others being seriously injured in the attempt to escape as the liner wallowed onto her side and came to rest on the rocky bed.

What happened next shocked everybody. Captain Schettino left the ship and all her occupants and saved himself in a lifeboat. A phone call to the coastguard was interesting to hear and made front pages around the world as the excuse he made was that he had 'fallen into a lifeboat'. The response was a barrage of obscenities and he was ordered back on board to assist with the rescue. Schettino did not go back on board and instead headed for shore.

As daylight broke the next day, the sight of the wreck of the *Costa Concordia* lying on her side next to a quaint little Italian harbour was surreal. A final count of people on board over the next few days revealed that thirty-two people were either dead or unaccounted for. The investigation immediately found the cause of the disaster was the reckless behaviour of the captain, now nicknamed 'Captain Coward' by the press. He was arrested and put on trial for manslaughter and causing a shipwreck.

Following a trial where Moldavian dancer Domnica Cemortan admitted that she had been Schettino's lover and was on the ship without a ticket while he was showing her the bridge, he was found guilty in February 2015 and jailed for sixteen years. He appealed his sentence, but this was rejected. Other members of the crew were tried and jailed for their part in the shipwreck, but this was little comfort to those who had died on what should have been a holiday cruise.

After the sinking a huge operation began to remove what was now the largest shipwreck in the world. Veteran salvage company Smit International, along with Italian firm NERI SpA, devised a plan to build a platform next to the vessel and, when ready, the *Costa Concordia* would be slowly pulled over and, if all went well, land upright on the platform. This took place straight away with the removal of hazardous materials such as her fuel and any other dangers that might hamper the operation. Over the space of several days in September 2013 she was once again successfully righted although still sunken up to her main deck. By this point the starboard side of the ship was now exposed and the damage of twenty months lying against the rocks was visible.

The next stage of the salvage was to raise the ship. This was easier said than done after a diver died while cutting a piece of sheet metal, reminding everyone just how dangerous this job was, even when the hardest part was already done.

In July 2014, after over two and a half years years on the rocks, the *Costa Concordia* was successfully refloated and was finally towed away to Genoa where investigators could begin the search for evidence and the missing. The final body was located in November that year.

By May 2015, the dismantling of the wreck began but it would take a staggering two years to complete before the ship was finally gone. Haunting photographs were released of the abandoned entertainment areas displaying the eeriness of a liner that was meant to provide fun and relaxation, but instead became a symbol of disaster and heartache.

Chapter 50

Unknown Migrant Vessel, 2015

The final shipwreck in this book is probably one of the most tragic sinkings of recent years, one that still remains anonymous today as do most of the people who died in the event. It stems back to the rumours rife in Africa that just across the Mediterranean is a world of success just waiting for them. With promises of work and a better life, thousands of migrants leave their villages, towns and cities to make the dangerous journey to the coast, places like Libya, often paying thousands of dollars to secure their position on a boat that will sneak them in through the back door. What most of them do not realize is that the friendly helpers who promise a better life are criminals, human traffickers, exploiting those with nothing and who care less for these people than they do for the rubber boats they cram them into. As groups of them arrive on the beaches and hide for days at a time, at some point a boat will pick them up and they will proceed north towards the coast of Europe where they hope to be welcomed with open arms. The truth is that what awaits them is a detention centre, migrant camps, long paperwork trails and most likely a ticket back to their original country.

These small boats are risky to take to sea, especially for such a long journey of hundreds of miles. The lifejackets alone are useless most of the time, the boats are barely seaworthy and it is quite common for over a hundred people to sit precariously on a rubber dinghy designed for a dozen at the most. In the years leading up to 2015, there had been an increase in the number of these journeys, with many of the boats sinking within a day, or capsizing and throwing the occupants into the water with no hope of rescue.

By now thousands of migrants had died, the seas around the south of Italy littered with bodies and buoyancy aids that had failed as life-saving devices. Every navy in Europe had deployed at least one ship to the region and various charities had hired their own ships to assist with rescues.

On 18 April 2015, an old fishing boat that no longer had a name, set sail from the port of Zuwarah near Tripoli, Libya. At the helm was Mohammed Ali Malek and Mahmud Bikhit who had loaded hundreds of desperate migrants into the hold below. Where it would have normally been used to stow fish or equipment, it is now thought to have had up to 800 people inside, crammed in so they could barely move. The dangerously overloaded boat, just 90 feet long, was slowly pushed out to sea on the single propeller, the two smugglers knowing that it wouldn't be long until the boat would be in peril.

Sure enough, water was already starting to seep into the boat and panic was setting in amongst those trapped below decks. Satisfied that they were now in international waters, a distress call was sent out for any ship in the area to come and pick them up. A nearby containership, the *King Jacob*, answered the call and sped to the scene. What greeted them was a tiny vessel that suddenly steered towards the huge ship and rammed into the port side. Whether they were trying to deliberately sink the boat or if it was just an accident, nobody can be too sure, but this was the end of the line for the vessel. With so many people on board, it simply rolled over and within five minutes had completely sunk. The suddenness was shocking. The crew of the *King Jacob* managed to rescue a pitiful twenty-eight survivors, the two smugglers amongst them.

The disaster opened the eyes of the world onto this body of water that was now the scene of yet another disaster, but this one was described as the worst loss of life in a Mediterranean shipwreck since the Second World War. Despite a search for survivors, none were found and the few who had been picked up were taken away for treatment and interviewing.

What was found out later was just how many people that boat had carried: it was a miracle it had got as far as it had. The two smugglers were arrested and put on trial for manslaughter in the Sicilian city of Catania. Malek was found to have been at the helm and was sentenced to eighteen years in jail and a 9-million-euro fine; his first mate Bikhit was handed a five-year sentence for people smuggling and also given a fine of €9 million.

The situation in the Mediterranean became a hot topic for European governments as the death toll was now too large to ignore, even though the past few years had seen a steadily increasing death rate – even the week before, there had been sinkings with over 400 dead.

The authorities now had to recover the wreck and find out if there were any bodies still on board. Divers duly located the wreck and a salvage team began to get into position to lift the vessel from the seabed. In June 2016, over a year after the disaster, with great care the small fishing boat was lifted up and broke the surface, being allowed to be drained of water before being hoisted onto a barge to be taken over to the Sicilian naval base of Melilli. It was here that the hold was finally opened up and the true horror of what had happened was exposed. Inside were 458 bodies, each having to be removed and attempts made at identification. Added to the bodies found in the water over the course of the weeks after the sinking, the official death toll stands at 675, with many others believed to have been swept out to sea and lost forever.

After the salvage and recovery was complete, the migrant boat took on a surprising and controversial journey when it was used by Swiss-Icelandic artist Christoph Buchel as a display piece in the city of Venice. Known as the Barca Nostra project (Our Ship), it is thought it will soon end up as a memorial in the town of Augusta, but not before people can look upon its hull and see for themselves the simple wooden boat that had cost so many lives in yet another tragic attempt to find a better life.

This boat will not be the last major migrant disaster; even as I write, more people are dying in the Mediterranean in yet other small-boat capsizes. Each one ends not only lives but the hopes and dreams of all that was carried, much to the frustration of those trying to help save them from certain death and a wasted journey. With so many unknown victims of this trade in human beings, it is an endless task to control the criminals that bring death and misery to the very seas that offer their victims hope.

Epilogue

As you might appreciate, it is difficult to select only fifty shipwrecks to talk about – I could easily have made this a hundred and fifty. There are so many more amazing stories out there – stories of survival, heroism, treasure, mystery and tragedy.

If I were to write a follow-up to this, then I would once again be stuck with which ones to include, but at the top of the list would be the loss of the troopship *Birkenhead* off the coast of South Africa in 1852. What is incredible about this particular loss is that while the women and children were being evacuated, the soldiers stood to attention and would not board the lifeboats until all those who could be saved had left the stricken ship: 450 of them died, but their actions would forever be known as the 'Birkenhead Drill' and they will always be remembered for their bravery. Then there is the Spanish ship *Nuestra Senora de Atocha*, lost off the Florida coast in 1622 loaded with treasure. It was the perseverance of a man named Mel Fisher that eventually found the wreck and all her riches after a search lasting sixteen years that had already cost the lives of his wife, son and a diver in a boat accident.

So, while we read about the fifty shipwrecks that I have chosen, remember there are three *million* wrecks worldwide. Each one has its own story, each has real people affected by the loss of the vessel, cargo and crew. No disaster should be forgotten and it has always been my intention to get as many on record as possible. The wrecks I have already covered in other books include the loss of HMS *Duchess* in a collision off Scotland, the *SRN6-012* hovercraft off Portsmouth and the tanker *Pacific Glory* just a few miles away. Gathering the information together and putting together the pieces of the jigsaw into a coherent story is a painstaking and sometimes frustrating task. Parts of the puzzle are always missing, people are no longer around to tell their version and things get lost over time, but as long as people are willing to go on record, there is hope that many more will be highlighted and, hopefully, memorials to these tragedies will forever honour those who died and, more importantly, those who made the ultimate sacrifice so that others may live.

Also by Richard M. Jones

The Great Gale of 1871
Lockington: Crash at the Crossing
The Burton Agnes Disaster
End of the Line: The Moorgate Disaster
Capsized in the Solent: The SRN6-012 Hovercraft Disaster
Royal Victoria Rooms: The Rise and Fall of a Bridlington Landmark
The Diary of a Royal Marine: The Life and Times of George Cutcher
Boleyn Gold (fiction)
Collision in the Night: The Sinking of HMS Duchess
RMS Titanic: The Bridlington Connections
Austen Secret (fiction)
Living the Dream, Serving the Queen
When Tankers Collide: The Pacific Glory Disaster
The Farsley Murders
Britain's Lost Tragedies Uncovered